WE ARE
IN THIS
TOGETHER

WE ARE
IN THIS
TOGETHER

Reflections on the Dramas of Life

Richard Stark

WE ARE IN THIS TOGETHER
Reflections on the Dramas of Life

Copyright 2021 by Richard Stark
All rights reserved

Published by: Work
Isbn:
pb: 978-1-956876-72-7
ebook: 978-1-956876-71-0

Bible verse [James 5:12] at the conclusion of "A Father's Legacy" is from the King James Version

To my mother and father

Contents

Excerpts, San Francisco Book Review
Introduction

Group I
Family and Friendship
--A Father's Legacy
--An Army of One
--The Treasure of a Friend
--A Mother's Gifts
--Home to Wisconsin

Group II
Citizenship and Country
--Day of Infamy
--We the People

Group III
Experience and Perspective
--A Journey in Time

Group IV
The Spirit of Adventure
--A Florida Adventure

Afterword
San Francisco Book Review (complete)
Notes

WE ARE IN THIS TOGETHER
Reflections on the Dramas of Life
by Richard Stark

Excerpts from … The San Francisco Book Review, 2014

"A thoughtful, meditative work."

"Captures the joy and sorrow felt throughout life."

"Tactful as well as enlightening."

"Abounds with wisdom and understanding."

"Grasps the monumental aspects of life."

"Earning four stars, it demonstrates a true appreciation for the path each individual must explore."

"Accessible to every reader and worth re-reading over the years."

Introduction

Dear gentle Reader,

These vignettes, or brief stories, were originally sent to family and friends at Christmastime—one annually, beginning in 2006, the year my father passed away.

Each vignette concerns a significant personal event or experience—my father's passing; our son's first deployment to Iraq; the loss of a lifelong friend; the subsequent loss of my mother; a visit home to Wisconsin; the anniversary of 9/11; a fortieth high school reunion; an observation regarding our US Constitution; and a bicycle journey to Florida—which others may relate to also. That is to say, each has a universal theme.

Except for the first vignette, regarding the death of my father, each begins with a question. The question alludes to the universal theme.

The universal themes are in four groups, and the stories appear chronologically, with the exception of "**A Journey in Time.**"

I hope you enjoy the stories.

Richard Stark
June 2021

Group I

Family and Friendship

"This fast-paced society of ours offers many fleeting attractions. There is not much, it seems, that is permanent—but family endures. That is to say, our relationships, with our loved ones and friends, are what matter in the end and what we come back to."

—From **"A Father's Legacy"**

A Father's Legacy

Friday, November 17, 2006

To: Cheri, Walt, Mike, Sharon, Maria, Diane, Craig, Antonio, Ava, Samantha, Carolyn, and Kari-Lyn

Subject: Thank you

Dear Shipmates (or as Craig aptly put it recently in an e-mail—"Shiftmates"):

Thank you each for your condolences regarding my father's passing on Wednesday. For what it's worth, here are a few thoughts so far. For those of you who have had a similar occurrence in your lives, perhaps we can compare notes.

My first impression: A degree of shock—like being pushed into a swimming pool unexpectedly. One's life has changed, and behold, the great mystery—*death*—presents itself. It's an "in-your-face" kind of thing.

The next morning: It appears to be just another day. The earth turns, impassively, the weather is unconcerned. The trees, the surroundings, all the same. It becomes oddly apparent—life simply, indifferently, goes on.

Now ahead is the funeral, on Monday. It certainly will be peculiar to see my father lying in a casket. In September my folks celebrated their sixty-fifth wedding anniversary.
I will be wondering what thoughts are going through my mother's mind.

Well, there is no stopping this. No ignoring or denying it. So we will travel to Wisconsin, my family and I, to attend.

Thank you all again for your kindness.

Richard

Friday, December 1, 2006

To: Cheri, Walt, Mike, Sharon, Maria, Diane, Craig, Antonio, Ava, Samantha, Carolyn, and Kari-Lyn

Subject: Follow-up

Dear Shipmates,

Regarding my father's funeral, thank you all for the lovely plant my mother received, and for the beautiful cards, and for your thoughts and prayers. Life has pretty much returned to normal now.

The funeral service on November 20th was very nice. In addition to relatives, some of my dad's golfing buddies and former colleagues attended.

My father served in World War II, so the local VFW honor guard was at the graveside with a twenty-one-gun salute and "Taps."

The weather cooperated nicely. It was a sunny, pleasant day.

My overall impression of the experience: This fast-paced society of ours offers many fleeting attractions. There is not much, it seems, that is permanent—but family endures. That is to say, our relationships, with our loved ones and friends, are what matter in the end and what we come back to.

Thank you all again.

Sincerely,
Richard

*One year earlier:
September 27, 2005*

It seemed strange to be dialing the new digits. For over fifty years, and my entire life up to this point, the home phone number for my parents had not changed—until recently, when my brothers and I helped Mom and Dad move into an assisted-living center. Now they had a different number. It was odd not to be entering the ever-so-familiar one, the one I had grown up with, the one that was for so long a part of each of our lives.

Dad answered on the third ring. "Hello."

Isn't it intriguing that, besides having unique fingerprints and other features, our voices are each different as well?

"Hi, Dad. Happy anniversary."

And isn't it remarkable the extent to which a person's voice, particularly that of a loved one, touches our lives?

"Thank you. Your mother isn't here. She's …" There was a pause. Dad had grown frail, and now, at age eighty-eight, conversing required some effort. "… at Bible Study, so …" Another pause. "I'll tell her when she comes in."

Although Dad's voice had weakened as his strength and stamina had declined over the years, it was still the familiar sound that had been in my life since my earliest memories.

"All right. And I hope you're having a wonderful day."

Learning to ride a bicycle. Working in our garden. Weekend walks in the woods. The voice had been there.

"The weather's nice. Just like it was … sixty-four years ago."

The reference was to September 27, 1941, the day Mom and Dad were married.

"It's beautiful here, too." I tried to imagine the view out the window there in Wisconsin, testing my memory of the climate. "You've got, what, sunshine and...seventy degrees?"

"I don't know what we have for temperature ... but the sun is shining."

Shoveling snow together. Ice fishing. Supper every night at five o'clock. So many memories of home and growing up, so many of which included the voice on the other end of the line.

"That sounds good. And Mom's at Bible Study. Well, any advice for us"—I tried to think of a fitting term—"young whippersnappers who have only been married for twenty-four years?"

As a practical, down-to-earth person, Dad had been, through the years, an ever reliable source of guidance and reason. Perhaps he had a gem to pass along this special day, as well.

"No."

We spoke then about Robin, who was training with the Army, at Fort Benning, Georgia. Robin had fractured his wrist, Marcy and I had recently learned, and Dad asked about, and we discussed, the circumstances of the injury.

Then we returned to the occasion at hand—Mom and Dad's wedding anniversary. I was still hoping for some sage words.

"So you don't have any advice for us younger group? You have sixty-four years to draw from. Give us a word of wisdom."

We often spend a lot of time interacting, with family, friends, and acquaintances, yet devote very little of it sharing what we have learned about that which is most meaningful in our lives. Sometimes, though, there are moments that surpass the everyday interaction. This became one of them.

"We still don't have all the answers."

Dad's response, though simple and brief, struck me as profound. And it gave me something to work with.

"So the advice is, hang in there, and keep searching for answers?"

There is a Scripture verse urging simplicity and integrity in one's speech—to "let your yea be yea; and *your* nay, nay;" That was Dad.

"That's about it."

Thought:
We can never repay all that our parents do for us
throughout our formative years.
We can only pass it on
when we are parents ourselves.

"At 0430 local time, his deployment in Iraq over, Robin and his fellow soldiers arrive at the Honolulu International Airport.
Our prayers for a safe return have been answered.
We are grateful."

—From **"An Army of One"**

An Army of One
2007

*Isn't it good to be reunited with
a loved one after an extended period of separation?*

It's a sunny Thursday morning in March. We are driving from our home in northern Virginia to nearby Reagan National Airport, adjacent the Potomac River near Washington DC. Robin, who is on active duty with the Army, and who has been deployed to Iraq for seven months in support of Operation Iraqi Freedom, is arriving home for fifteen days of leave.

I drop Marcy and Alexandra at the walkway in front of the airport terminal. As arranged, they go to meet Robin in the baggage area. Meanwhile, I pull away to establish a holding pattern. Driving past the cell phone waiting area and leisurely continuing, I note the traffic signs directing one back to the terminal. I return once, twice.

On the third approach, there he is—the light gray camouflage of his Army Combat Uniform incongruous with the external airport surroundings. Broad-shouldered, erect in his carriage and confident in his stride, our Army of One appears the epitome of fitness.

I pull up, stop, and pop the trunk for Robin's luggage—a large, green duffle bag. It is tightly packed, and heavy, I discover, as, during greetings, I briefly struggle to maneuver it into the trunk space. Then I receive a firm hug—and omigod, such solid musculature of arms and chest! Twenty-four years old, 190 pounds, Army trained, combat ready—and as healthy and fit as one can be.

I am released, and as I climb back into the driver's seat, I marvel at his strength, his youth, his vitality.

"I can't believe how fast we're going."

It's Robin speaking. We're on the highway, driving home. We are matching the general traffic flow.

Robin explains.

Duties in Iraq include frequent missions. The mode of transportation for him and his platoon is an armored Humvee. Due to the ever-present danger of encountering an insurgent-planted improvised explosive device, or IED, and in order to maintain an effective lookout, the Humvee is driven at no more than twenty miles per hour during the day, and half that at night.

Pondering this, one can understand that, after months of conducting missions under such restricted driving conditions, sixty-five miles per hour on the open highway would indeed seem a very fast pace.

We are home, and our family is complete. Lianne is back from work and Robin has settled in. He has eaten, showered after his long journey, and has accessed his duffle bag to transition to casual shirt and jeans. He looks almost like a teenager again.

Robin spends a few days at home. He enjoys a carefree weekend. Operation Iraqi Freedom becomes temporarily distant as he relaxes and recuperates. He sleeps late. He has friends to visit, and a social life once again to pursue.

On the Monday following his arrival, Robin and his longtime best friend from high school, a friendly, outgoing Muslim named Masood whose family is from Afghanistan, travel together to vacation in the Bahamas. They spend a week partaking of sun, sea, and tropical nightlife.

During Robin's absence, Marcy and I, too, are on leave, of sorts. Gone is the anxiousness of the last seven months, and the parental concern for our son's safety.

It's a welcome reprieve.

Robin's leave ends, and he returns to Iraq. His year-long deployment is initially due to end in August. We learn that his battalion is being extended up to ninety days.

Robin responds intermittently to e-mails. He calls home from time to time. And, along with the other families, we receive updates from the battalion commander, informing us of the progress being made in combating the Iraqi insurgency and improving the security of the local populace. The commander writes with heartfelt admiration of the unwavering professionalism of our soldiers enduring trying conditions.

We look forward to the day when their time in Iraq draws to a close.

The news comes, finally, in October. Robin phones home for Marcy's birthday.

It's three o'clock in the morning in Iraq and he has just returned from his final mission. Replacements have been arriving and are taking over. Soon the entire battalion will have departed, flying to Kuwait and then on to Hawaii and their duty station at Schofield Barracks.

The news is the nicest birthday present Marcy could ask for.

A week later we learn that Marcy's birthday present is complete. At 0430 local time, his deployment in Iraq over, Robin and his fellow soldiers arrive at the Honolulu International Airport.

Our prayers for a safe return have been answered.

We are grateful.

Thought:
Our soldiers, sailors, airmen, marines,
and Coast Guard personnel
—all who serve in uniform—
deserve our perpetual respect and gratitude.

Dedication

*To the eighteen valiant young men of Robin's unit—
soldiers of the*

*2nd Battalion, 27th Infantry Regiment
—The Wolfhounds—*

*who died while serving in support of
Operation Iraqi Freedom.*

*May God forever bless their families
and keep them in His care.*

"But how fortunate to have had such a once-in-a-lifetime comrade and confidant in a fellow human being. What a treasure it has fashioned. What a storehouse of memories remain. What a blessing to have known such enduring qualities of true friendship—in a world that can be fickle and harsh."

—From **"The Treasure of a Friend"**

The Treasure of a Friend
2008

Have you ever met somebody, and it seemed as though you'd known the person all your life?

It was the summer of 1975, during college. I had a job as a lifeguard, was off duty for two days, and was returning from visiting my folks, having hitchhiked the approximately hundred miles home the day before. I was in the Wisconsin Dells area, just north of my destination of Devil's Lake State Park and the tiny cabin I was renting for the summer.

It was a sunny day, warm and humid. The rides had been good, but now I found myself semistranded along Highway 12. The tourist traffic of the Dells area apparently was just not as hitchhiker-friendly as the rest of rural, southern Wisconsin.

Until finally, a car pulled over and stopped. I had no way of knowing it at the time, but I was about to meet my best friend of the next thirty-three years.

His name was Victor Ramsey. He was a lifelong bachelor in his early fifties, thirty years my senior. He was not a large man—his height was below average, his frame slender, with a bespectacled appearance that was neat and tidy. He didn't normally pick up hitchhikers, not since a
bad experience some years earlier, when his generosity in giving a lift to his fellow man resulted in an attempted carjacking.

However, when he spied me with my thumb out and

discerned a nonthreatening demeanor, he allowed himself to make an exception to his rule. It was a comment I heard with some frequency on the road: "I don't normally pick up hitchhikers, but you looked clean-cut and respectable, so I decided to stop."

We drove and talked. My ride had a rare authenticity about him, devoid of any pretense. He was a workingman, as down to earth as one could be. He had grown up on a farm in the area, the younger of several siblings. He had lived in Milwaukee for more than twenty years, eventually deciding to return to the rural area of his roots. He was kind enough to drop me off almost at my doorstep, my little cabin being among those at the corner of County DL and Old Lake Road, comprising a quiet haven called Silverdale Resort—my home for the summer.

Isn't it interesting how a single, seemingly chance circumstance can affect our lives?

I had enjoyed meeting the affable Mr. Ramsey. Apparently the thought was mutual. When I returned from work the next day, I found a note on my cabin door from my new acquaintance, inviting me to give a call.

I did, and soon after we enjoyed a genial dinner together, with Mr. Ramsey—Vic—as host. I was introduced to his specialty—home-cooked pot roast. It was superb.

In spite of the difference in our ages, we easily related. And although Vic got along well by himself—there had been a prospective lady friend at one point, but it never became serious—it did get lonely for him. But now, by way of a serendipitous encounter on the road, a remarkable friendship had begun to form, one that would significantly enhance both of our lives.

How does one summarize over three decades of memories? Vic became more than a friend. He was like family.

The following summer he invited me to upgrade my standard of living, and share accommodations in his clean, comfortable, two-bedroom condo. He helped me get a job in the factory where he worked, as I continued to lifeguard on weekends. Weekdays we commuted to work together, and during our lunch breaks frequently retreated to his car to rest, eat our sandwiches, and listen to Paul Harvey on the radio.

Vic's longtime coworkers and former lunch mates observed this curious revision to his bachelor routine, and as the summer progressed, one finally asked him, pointblank and good-naturedly, "What is he, your illegitimate son?"

The query became for us a lifelong source of humor.

Time passed.

I finished school. Joined the Navy. Was stationed overseas on a ship.

Vic and I kept in touch throughout.

During my time overseas—I was stationed for two years on an aircraft carrier homeported in Japan—Vic was a living link to my own Wisconsin roots. He sent letters, and occasional tapes of my favorite music, recorded off the radio. He would add his own narrative, of news, humor, and inspirational quotes and passages. One Christmas, spent at sea, there arrived from my friend a small package containing a green, needle-covered sprig from a Wisconsin
pine. It became for my shipmates and me a tiny Christmas tree in our bunkroom.

After meeting Marcy, transferring to Hawaii for four years of duty ashore at Pearl Harbor, and getting married there and starting a family, Vic traveled twice to visit. He became a second father-in-law to Marcy, and an additional grandparent to Robin and Lianne—and later, Alexandra. He watched them grow and was involved in the process. In Wisconsin, after a third and final tour of duty, once again in Japan, and for three years ashore, we were next-door neighbors for a time.

By now, Vic considered us his family, just as much as he was part of ours.

And indeed, it was so.

More time passed.

Vic retired. The condo was sold. There was a transition to a tidy, one-bedroom apartment.

Vic grew elderly, and I became middle-aged—a few years older, in fact, than Vic was when we first met.

We could reminisce now, about memories long past ...

"Hey Vic, remember ...

... that Christmas break in college, when it was below zero and the heater in your car wasn't working, and we all but froze driving to work in the morning?"

... driving to Florida and stopping for gas, and I suggested we look under the hood, and you asked why, and I said I read somewhere that during a long trip it's good to check the engine in case anything is loose—so you popped the hood and lifted it up, and called out: "ANYTHING LOOSE IN THERE?"

... camping near the Everglades, and the raccoons were so pesky that we didn't dare walk away from the picnic table or they'd be all over our food—and when they just wouldn't leave us alone, you finally got so aggravated that you started throwing things at them?"

... in Hawaii on the Big Island, when Robin was only two, and we wanted to see the Green Sand Beach that we had heard about, and we found it on the map and it was miles from the roadway—so after parking the car the three of us starting hiking to it, while Marcy stayed behind with infant Lianne—and then Robin got tired, so the two of you started back, and then you carried him and he fell asleep—and when Marcy saw you returning with Robin limp in your arms, she thought something terrible had happened to us and that Robin was dead?"

Isn't it nice to reminisce?

Doesn't it bring a smile, recalling special moments shared? Doesn't it warm the heart?

Aren't the simplest times often those we remember most fondly?

And isn't it nice to have that next phone call to look forward to? The next visit to anticipate? That next time to be together?

And wouldn't it be good, if it could always be so?

The news came very unexpectedly, in a phone call from Vic's niece, Sharon Peterson.

We learned that Vic had been taken to the hospital. That he had collapsed, and had been discovered by a neighboring tenant, extremely weak. That a large mass had been diagnosed, and an internal infection. That his condition had deteriorated further during the night.

And that—his blood pressure low, pulse weak, respiration decreasing—with Sharon at his bedside, he had quietly passed away.

***

It's been some weeks now, since we got the news.

Vic's remains have been cremated. A memorial service is pending.

How unusual that I can no longer pick up the phone, enter Vic's number, and speak with my friend.

How odd to think that we won't hear his voice again.

How different will the trips to Wisconsin be, without Vic there to visit.

And—after all these years and the many moments Vic was part of, and after all the laughter shared—how very, very strange to know that our interaction on this planet has ended. What a lasting void that creates.

But how fortunate to have had such a once-in-a-lifetime comrade and confidant in a fellow human being. What a treasure it has fashioned. What a storehouse of memories remain. What a blessing to have known such enduring qualities of true friendship—in a world that can be fickle and harsh.

From each of us, Vic—thank you so much.

We miss you. We will remember you.

God bless you, dear friend.

Thought:
With family and friends,
laughter
is love, having fun.

"Someday, years hence, the house would be quiet on these winter mornings, with weekends that were leisurely and carefree. Today, though, life consisted of long underwear in boys' sizes, flannel shirts and corduroy trousers, and sweaters, scarves, coats, caps, mittens, and snow boots."

—From **"A Mother's Gifts"**

A Mother's Gifts
2009

*Is there anyone in our lives who
deserves to be revered more than our mother?*

I am so glad I phoned home to Wisconsin on Saturday, January 17th.

It had been a few weeks since my last call and conversation with Mom. During that time there had been a nagging thought, persistent in reminding me that I was overdue in giving Mom a call. So on impulse that day I took a moment, picked up the phone, and entered Mom's number. I'll be forever thankful that I did.

Our conversation turned out to be the last one.

Three days later, on Tuesday, January 20th, after a three-and-a-half-year battle with multiple myeloma, and after well outlasting the prognosis Mom had initially been given when diagnosed, that she had perhaps a year, maybe two, and having decided some months earlier to minimize further treatment, electing instead to let Nature take its course, Mom peacefully experienced the end she had been bravely facing for many months, and which she had come not to fear, rather for which she had told us she was ready, and in fact, welcomed.

This is the first Christmas without Mother.

But on Christmas morning, when it's time to open the presents, and, bleary-eyed from Christmas Eve and Midnight Mass and the extra late bedtime which unavoidably results, and when sleeping in becomes an appealing option which inevitably gives way to the impatient promptings of those already up, and when groggily descending the stairs to join the clamor and, disheveled and hungry, taking one's place on the couch and surveying the scene—lighted tree sparkling, colorfully wrapped gifts being handed out, and familiar faces in attendance—it can be observed that yet under the tree are three gifts remaining.

They are from Mother.

They are there every Christmas—and have been, for all the Christmases I can remember.

The first is the largest of the three. It is golden.
It is the gift of Life.

Behold, the gift ...

I am but a speck, and my earthly existence has just begun. A moment ago, I didn't exist at all.

Now I am a single cell. I am a zygote—and the process is underway.

Moments become days as, hidden and protected, in this warm and special place, I'm growing.

Soon I have arms, legs, a tiny beating heart.

The growing continues, and then one day, at the appointed hour, ready to leave warmth and security behind, I transition to a sudden shock of cold.

What is THIS? My lungs begin their work as, naked and distressed, I protest the discomfort.

Soon, though, discomfort ends. I am wrapped, and warm once again.

The ordeal is nearly over. I'm here.

And all at once, so tired.

So I sleep.

Sunshine
blue sky   clouds drifting   warm, soft sand   ocean surf

Dawn breaking
pink horizon   pristine lake   glassy calmness
fish jumps   silence reigns

Springtime
gentle breeze   birds singing   green grass, flowers, trees
blossoms bursting   world anew

Summer sidewalk
time suspended   busy anthill   world in miniature
silent spectacle   mystery in endless motion

Autumn leaves
crisp air   geese flying, pointed south   drama in flight
honking fades

Midwinter night
all aslumber   snow falling gently   Nature's art
morning sunshine   world of dazzling white

Evening solitude
clear, quiet night   vast, dark sky   myriad points of light
Eternity made visible

The second gift is almost the size of the first. It is crimson. It is the gift of Love.

Discomfort returns, with frequency.
I'm hungry. Or wet. Sometimes both.
I cry to announce my condition. It's my only voice.
And each time, the discomfort ends.
Gentle hands attend to me.
They feed me. They wash and wrap me. They keep me clean, and dry, and warm.
The hands lift me. I am rocked, and stroked, and cuddled.
And a voice speaks to me. I recognize the sound. I heard it, distant and muffled, when I was growing in the special place. The voice is tender, and soothing.
And eyes gaze deep into mine—as the hands hold me, and the voice coos my name.
I smile.
I am safe here—with the hands, and the eyes, and the voice.

Well. The focus here is a mother's gift of love.

So, a question: *If you were to provide a personal illustration of motherly sacrificial love—what would it be?*

It had been snowing heavily all night. By morning, the accumulation, on top of the already thick crust, was considerable. Wisconsin winter had come early. There was going to be a very white Christmas this year.

The boys, eager to experience the fresh snow, were already finishing their breakfast.

Their mother had been up before dawn. There were sandwiches to be made, and a Thermos of hot coffee to prepare. Sometimes the boys accompanied their father on his Saturday ice fishing trips and predawn departures. Then there would be additional sandwiches needed, and hot cocoa as well.

And then, for the mother, there would be a quiet day of focused activity and household chores.

On this morning, however, the first of the chores would be getting the boys bundled up and out the door. Then attention could be given to the cleaning that needed to be done, and the laundry that was waiting.

Someday, years hence, the house would be quiet on these winter mornings, with weekends that were leisurely and carefree. Today, though, life consisted of long underwear in boys' sizes, flannel shirts and corduroy trousers, and sweaters, scarves, coats, caps, mittens, and snow boots.

Thus attired, the boys herded to the door. There was a cold blast of air as they marched into the frigid temperature.

For the moment, all was quiet in the house.

Soon the beds were made, then the dishes done and the laundry gathered. The mother was well along with the vacuuming, and was unloading laundry, when there was a commotion at the door.

The boys were back—mittens, coats, and scarves crusted with snow, faces ruddy from the raw wind.

There was another icy blast as the door opened.

"We're freezing!" the boys exclaimed, as they stomped snow from their boots and trudged inside.

"We're ready to come back in now!"

The third gift is similar in size to the second. It is silver. It is the gift of Laughter.

My discomfort has become routine, and of little concern to me.

I've learned to trust the gentle hands, the soothing voice, and the eyes that peer into mine.

My interest now is in exploring my surroundings, and discovering my world.
I'm beginning to make use of my appendages.
My legs move awkwardly as I push and squirm. My arms move less awkwardly, and I'm gaining control of my hands and fingers.
I can grasp. I'm experiencing sizes, shapes, and textures. There seems no end to the variety.
As my world expands and my excitement grows, I discover within me a new sound.
It wells up inside and becomes ... a giggle.
It's a new form of expression. I use it often.
It feels good.

What is the funniest tale told in *your* family?

We had a cat growing up. We also had a pool table, in the downstairs area, in what was called the recreation, or rec room.

Some pool tables have drop pockets, usually of leather mesh, in which the balls accumulate until retrieved.

Ours, however, was constructed with a gully system—an enclosed conduit, or channel, running the length of the table on either side, with a slight degree of downward slope to the head, or front. This was a convenient feature which gently harnessed gravity, and which served to retrieve the balls automatically during play. If, for instance, the **8 ball** was in motion, rolling across the table surface and dropping into an end corner pocket, it would proceed to travel forward inside the table, passing under the side pocket. When the ball reached the head corner pocket, it would be nearing the end of its journey, and would reappear at the head of the table below the playing surface, on a recessed groove designed to hold any of the fifteen solid or striped balls no longer in play.

Well, one night after bedtime, the following events occurred, which Mom would later relate:

Mom and Dad were down in the rec room. Dad was at the pool table, and the sounds had attracted the attention of the cat. She had sprung up onto the table and had become intrigued as the balls disappeared into the pockets. She began reaching into the openings, swiping with a paw as they rolled away.

This, in turn, became a little game for Dad and the cat, with Mom as spectator.

The method of play was simple. Dad, positioned at a head corner pocket, and with a flick of the wrist in the opening, would roll a pool ball up inside the table to the side pocket, where the cat was poised to swat at it with her paw.

Once begun, the game continued, back and forth—Dad rolling the ball, and the cat swatting it back.

Eventually, Dad decided to stop—it was late and time for bed.

Sharing the story afterward with others, Mom would laugh robustly as she described what happened next:

Dad was casually making his way toward the stairs, intending to call it a night, when out of the blue he was attacked. It was the cat. She was angry, and wild.

And as Mom looked on, she witnessed Dad being chased around the pool table, as he attempted to evade the sharp claws.

The cat had never exhibited this kind of behavior before. The abrupt change was bewildering.

Then all at once it was obvious—she wanted to keep playing.

And sure enough, as soon as Dad repositioned himself at

the table, the cat relented, springing up once again to assume her place, as well.

And so the game continued—Dad rolling the ball to the cat, and the cat swatting it back.

It wasn't until the cat tired of the sport that Dad was allowed to retreat, ascend the stairs, and retire for the evening.

Thought:
A mother's love is pure.
And pure love
is the highest form
of creative energy.

In loving memory of
Beatrice Catherine Landwehr Stark

Mother: Thank you for the gifts, this Christmas and every year—and for a lifetime of godly example. God bless you always.

"We are, it seems, removed from civilization. Perhaps it was the circuitous drive and bumpy back road leading here that make it seem so. Or perhaps it is the simplicity of the immense vista before us."

—From "**Home to** *Wisconsin*"

Home to *Wisconsin*
2010

*As the weeks wind down and the year draws to a close,
isn't it nice to have memories that remain?*

Day One

It's late afternoon, mid-week in August. Alexandra and I are at Reagan National Airport, near our home in northern Virginia, and across the Potomac River from Washington DC. One of my favorite moments is about to occur—when tension subsides, calm descends, and all is serene.

    We have checked in for our flight. We have navigated through security. And, after a short walk through the terminal, we are arriving at our gate.

    There are passengers waiting. There are also seats available.

    As Ally and I claim ours and settle in, the moment arrives—life becomes simple and carefree.

    The task of packing for one's trip and loading the luggage has been completed. The stress of having a flight to catch—driving to the airport, shuttling to the terminal, arriving sufficiently ahead of time—is over. The need to check in and process through security has been met.

    There is nothing left to do at this point, except—sit back, relax ... and wait.

    The boarding call we are awaiting: Midwest Airlines Flight 1623, nonstop to Milwaukee.

    We are taxiing to the runway.

    Ally and I have seats 13A and 13B, on the port side of the aircraft. Ally has opted for the aisle seat. I have the window.

Ahead of us, as I crane my neck, the plane appears half full.

Outside, the weather is sunny and clear. As we taxi, I observe the airport activity. In the distance, the Washington Monument comes into view. Also visible is the Jefferson Memorial—and the dome of the US Capitol Building. I occupy myself by taking photos.

Ally asks for gum. We both take a piece. As we chew, the aircraft swings onto the runway. Moments later, engines at full power, we are pressed into our seats.

We are at our cruising altitude of thirty-four thousand feet. I'm gazing out the window.

The blue sky is pretty—as are the layers of cottony clouds below.

As we travel westward, the layers become patches, and, six miles down, vast areas of Mother Earth appear.

As always, when our mode of transportation is by air, I am impressed, even amazed, at the convenience of flying.

Driving to Wisconsin is a journey of two days, with an overnight stop in Indiana.

A direct flight, on the other hand, is all of two hours—barely enough time to rest, browse a magazine, and partake of the in-flight salad and sandwich options.

Soon, then, we begin our descent. As I watch the slow passing of the landscape far below, a large expanse of blue water appears, and we begin to cross Lake Michigan.

Shortly thereafter, in the distance, the Wisconsin shoreline becomes visible, and we prepare for landing.

It's early evening. We've claimed our luggage and are in the rental car garage, across the street from the airport terminal, ready for our vehicle.

My first preference, a Chevy Impala, is not available. I'm

offered a Chrysler 300, black in color. After a cursory look at the automobile, I sign the paperwork.

Ally and I stow our luggage and climb in. I start the engine, and we wend our way out of the garage to the airport roadway. At the highway, I accelerate and merge into traffic.

Our adventure has begun.

The Chrysler provides a smooth ride.

As we cruise westward on I-94 toward Madison, our destination, I explore the options on the radio. As might be inevitable, with Milwaukee receding in the distance behind us, I discover a station playing polka music.

"Ally!" I exclaim. "Polka music!"

Ally is eleven years old, from Virginia—and clearly not impressed.

"Eww! I feel like I'm in a room full of old people."

The sun is setting on our first day in Wisconsin. We make a stop en route, at Delafield.

It's something I've been anticipating since November 2008, when my best friend of thirty-three years and our longtime family friend, Vic Ramsey, passed away.

We want to visit Vic's niece, Sharon Peterson, who was with Vic at the time of his passing, and who contacted us with the news.

We're in luck. Sharon, and her husband, Duane, are home.

They welcome us in, with warm Midwest hospitality.

It's after dark, and our long day is coming to an end.

We arrive in Wisconsin's capital city, the home of my youngest brother, Terry, and his daughter, Gabriela, age seven, where we will stay.

We are soon settled in.

Day Two

Midwest summer morning.
Tranquil new day.
Blue sky. Sunshine.
Warm, fresh air.
Breakfast.
Then—towels, swimsuits, sandals, sunscreen—times four.
Sleek black Chrysler. Adventure mobile.
Scenic countryside. Peaceful drive.
Rolling meadows. Fields and forests.
Picturesque farmland. Rural serenity.
Small town America. Main Street, U.S.A.
Then—Wisconsin Dells, and a giant waterpark.

Perfect weather. Cloudless sky.
Bright warm sunshine.
Fun for all.
Giant pool. Big Kahuna.
Manmade waves. Throngs of bathers.
Adventure River. Crystal water.
Inner tubes, floating by.
Wade. Reach. Settle in.
Languid ride. Pleasant journey.
Floating.
Dozing.
Drift along.

*Humungous complex. Rides galore.
Pools, slides, fountains—more.
Family friendly.
Adventure too.
Black Anaconda. Stingray.
Scorpion's Tail. Flash Flood.
Dark Voyage. Time Warp.
Jungle Rapids. Kowabunga.
Curse of the Crypt.
Congo Bongo.
Lots of photos.
All-day fun.*

Day Three

It's the day after our visit to the Dells and *"America's Largest Waterpark."* Ally and I are once again northbound on scenic Highway 12. It's approaching dinnertime.

Our destination is the village of Roxbury and a favorite German restaurant there, the *Dorf Haus*. It's a quaint local establishment that has been in business for over half a century.

After a leisurely drive through the rural countryside, we arrive and find the main parking lot nearly full. We join a stream of other guests as they stroll to the entrance. Inside, the clamor of numerous conversations and the varied aromas of authentic German cuisine fill the air. We are without a reservation, and we learn that the wait time to be seated is ninety minutes. The friendly hostess graciously offers to add us to the waiting list. We accept, then return to the car.

We visit nearby Sauk City, along the Wisconsin River. After a stop at the Piggly Wiggly, we window shop along Water Street.

When we arrive back at the *Dorf Haus*, the crowd has thinned.

We are ushered to a cozy table. We order, and dinner is soon served.

It is worth the wait.

Day Four

The small waves ripple gently against the layer of rocks along the grassy lakefront. The sound is rhythmic, natural. I'm standing on the pier, watching the water, observing the motion.

It's early evening, the next day. Ally and I are at the tapered southern end of Big Cedar Lake, north of Milwaukee, visiting my younger brother, Bob. It's one of my favorite places—tranquil, stress-free, Mother Nature at her best.

In the late-day sunshine, the lake reflects the color of the cloudless blue sky. Year-round and summer homes, with their respective piers and swimming areas, ring the shoreline, and are nestled among tall oak and maple, pine and white birch trees.

In the distance, a powerboat turns sharply, the sound of its engine discordant over the water. The boat is towing a yellow ski tube. Two male bathers in life jackets, prone and side-by-side, cling to the multiple front handles, legs trailing in the water. The ski tube slows and partially submerges as the boat turns. Then, momentum building once again, the water churns and the bathers bounce and splash across the surface of the lake.

Near my location on the pier, a white swimming raft floats placidly. As the wake of the powerboat arrives, the raft, and the four flotation drums it rests upon, bob gently in the water.

Dusk begins to settle. I join my brother on the shore, as Ally explores nearby.

Bob has gathered an assortment of loose sticks and twigs. In a waterfront depression of blackened embers, he lights the dry wood. A small fire crackles. Thick white smoke curls upward toward the lake. I note the pleasant scent of wood smoke. As the flames grow, I feel the heat on my hands and face.

Darkness slowly descends—and our fourth day in Wisconsin comes quietly, peacefully, to a close.

Day Six

According to our highway map, the distance from Madison to Superior is 323 miles.

It's two days later, in the afternoon. Ally and I have departed Madison and are driving northward to Superior and the home of my elder brother, Jim. We will spend the night.

The weather is fair once again, making for a scenic, pleasant drive to the state's northernmost city.

We travel along Interstate 94. Three hours into the drive, we pass the halfway point. Then, at Eau Claire, we merge onto US Highway 53.

Traffic thins as we journey north. We begin to have miles of roadway to ourselves.

The time passes. Cruise control maintains a steady pace.

Ally watches movies on her portable DVD player. I reminisce about other trips to Superior. One in particular comes to mind. It was years earlier, with Robin and Lianne, and it included a singularly memorable event—that of observing black bears in their natural habitat.

It occurred at a small clearing in the Wisconsin Northwoods, thirty miles outside of Superior, along a rural dirt roadway. The clearing was used as a feeding site by an area farmer. The farmer, who periodically drove to the northwestern Wisconsin village of Poplar and a taco shell factory there, routinely hauled unusable, discarded taco shells back to the site—for the benefit of the local black bear population. Black bears frequented the site, feeding on the discarded shells. Word spread, and curious local residents, wanting to see the bears, also began to visit the site.

One evening at dusk, we joined a string of other vehicles parked along the roadway, opposite the site. We sat and waited. Before long, a small black bear emerged from the woods. Then another. Soon there were several, varying in size. We watched as the bears foraged about, undeterred by our vehicles and the occasional sound of a car door being quietly opened, as some onlookers discretely ventured closer.

For my brother Jim, who was our tour guide, it was a familiar sight. He had seen the bears before—including a particularly large one that sometimes appeared. For Robin, Lianne and me, though, it was an entirely new experience.

My reverie ends as we cruise along. I know we are nearing our destination when, up ahead, a large shape swoops low over the highway. It's a bald eagle, the white feathers of its head and tail clearly visible.

I alert Ally, and as she scrambles to pause her movie and get a glimpse, the eagle glides gracefully over the open landscape, disappearing into the tall trees beyond.

Day Seven

The following morning we are a party of six—including Jim, wife Cindy, daughter Michelle, and granddaughter Patriot—and we are standing on the quiet, far western shore of Lake Superior.

We are on *Wisconsin Point*—a narrow, three-mile-long peninsula of woods and wildlife, hiking trails and beach, and which, with its counterpart to the north, Minnesota Point, reportedly comprises the world's largest freshwater sand bar. The *"Point"* lies on the outskirts of Superior's city limits, and separates Lake Superior from Allouez Bay, and the city.

It's another pleasant summer day. The air is warm, with occasional sunshine through bluish overcast.

We are barefoot on the beach. Ally is in her swimming suit. It is tranquil, secluded, and we have the ribbon of sand to ourselves.

We are, it seems, removed from civilization. Perhaps it was the circuitous drive and bumpy back road leading here that make it seem so. Or perhaps it is the simplicity of the immense vista before us.

Lake Superior's vast, gray expanse extends to the horizon. To the north, far in the distance, a thin green line—the forested shore of Minnesota—arcs outward along the lake, as far as the eye can see. To the south extends the northwestern shoreline of Wisconsin.

There is no surf. The water is calm, and very shallow. There is almost no slope of the lake bed. Alexandra and Patriot, wading far from shore, are indistinguishable in the distance. Viewing them through my camera, employing full zoom, I can discern their features and see that the water is still only to their midsections.

We linger on the beach. I wander about, gathering a handful of smooth, rounded little stones. Alexandra and Patriot return to shore, rejoining our little group.

Soon our short-lived reunion will conclude. We will gather our things and follow the narrow path back to our vehicles. We will brush off the sand and prepare to depart. After our good-byes, Jim and family will drive home. Ally and I will return to Highway 53. We will journey south, with fresh memories of our sojourn to upper Wisconsin.

And, as we cruise along, we will look forward to our return.

Ally and I are back in Sauk City.

We are seated at a window booth in Culver's restaurant, adjacent the Piggly Wiggly. With its blue and white motif, the fast, casual restaurant—*Culver's ButterBurgers & Frozen Custard*—is one of four-hundred-plus locations throughout the Midwest and beyond. This particular site, opened in 1984, was the first.

We are reminiscing.

If our friend Vic Ramsey were alive, he would be with us today, ButterBurger in hand. Or we would order to go, and drive the short distance to his apartment near Water Street. We would enjoy the sunny summer day together, as we—Alexandra and I, and Robin and Lianne before her, and sometimes Marcy—did so many times over the years. Later today, or maybe tomorrow, we would visit nearby Devil's Lake State Park.

A thought comes to me.

Do our loved ones ever visit us from beyond the grave?

I share my thought with Ally. "I wonder if Vic is here with us," I say.

The comment is rhetorical. The answer will remain a mystery.

I regard the ButterBurger in my hand. With Ally observing, I speak for both of us.

"Vic," I announce, "this one's for you."

Day Eight

It's midmorning, a week after our arrival in Wisconsin.

Ally and I are southbound on US Highway 41, after visiting Bob a second time, and staying overnight at Big Cedar Lake.

We are driving to Milwaukee to relinquish our rental car, and check in for our return flight to Virginia.

There has been sunshine every day of our vacation—until today.

For the first time since we arrived, the sky is overcast and gray, and it's raining.

"Ally," I ask, "do you know why it's raining today?"

Ally looks over to me from the passenger seat. She waits for the answer.

"Because Wisconsin is sad that we're leaving."

Thought:
Truly, there is
no place like home.

Group II

Citizenship and Country

*"The enemy struck on September 11th. Each of us was affected. Now we are all in this together.
Such is the sense of unity in the air. It is palpable—a feeling of oneness, a patriotic kinship unlike anything I've known."*

—From **"Day of Infamy"**

Day of Infamy
September 11, 2001
Ten-Year Anniversary
2011

What are your *recollections and impressions of the morning, and aftermath, of 9/11?*

Part I – The Attack

It's morning, the second Tuesday of September.
  My schedule is such that I'm off from work, not to return until the next day. I enjoy the luxury of sleeping in, there being no compelling reason to do otherwise.
  The day starts lazily around nine o'clock, and finds me sometime after padding semigroggily through the living room.
  Our two-year-old, Alexandra, is up and, as usual, is engrossed in her Cartoon Network on television. She pays me little mind as I pass by. Her grandmother is in the kitchen, which is my destination, when the phone rings. I answer it in the living room. It's Marcy, calling from work.
  "Hon, did you hear the news?" A sense of urgency in my

wife's voice dispels any lingering grogginess on my part.

"What happened?" I'm not sure I want to know. It's unusual for Marcy to be phoning this early in the day, and her tone is serious. What in the world has occurred? A tornado? An earthquake? A tsunami?

"Two airliners flew into the World Trade Center in New York. Turn on the T.V."

I locate the remote, preempting Ally's usual programming. She doesn't protest, which is out of character for her. Usually there is no competing with her insistent rallying cry: "I want my own show!" Does she sense, perhaps, something is amiss? Why is Daddy concerned?

Remote in hand, the image in the living room changes from animated characters and dubbed voices to billowing black smoke and the World Trade Center's twin towers.

Shock. Disbelief.

Unable to account for such an unimaginable live scenario, the mind goes blank. There is little conversation as, receiver to my ear, my wife and I share the passing moments. Then, without warning, the boundary of disbelief is pushed further.

"Oh my God, Hon," I hear myself saying, "one of the towers is collapsing!"

It quickly becomes official: the United States has experienced a terrorist attack of unprecedented magnitude.

The Federal Aviation Administration responds, suspending all commercial flight activity. And then, for the first time in memory, and after decades of observing them in the skies high overhead, there are no vapor trails across America.

The rest of the morning, and most of the afternoon, is spent transfixed by the breaking story.

Two scenes become indelibly ingrained upon the mind, appearing repeatedly as they are rebroadcast again and again. The first is that of a Boeing 767 airliner gliding like a missile toward one of the towering structures, while the other stands already in flames. The airliner disappears into concrete and steel. There follows, again and again, the inevitable fireball.

The second set of footage is that of black smoke and the towers collapsing.

First the one.

Then, like a loyal twin unwilling to allow its dear sibling to meet a terrible fate alone, the other.

Meanwhile, thirty miles north of our Virginia home, the Pentagon is in flames and smoke. And an airliner has crashed into a field in Pennsylvania.

Upon awakening the next morning, one wonders if it was all just a nightmare.

But then, grim reality settles.

And in the days that follow, it becomes apparent how closely the terrorism has struck.

When the smoke clears at the Pentagon, the name of a coworker's husband is on the missing list. He is later confirmed dead.

Lianne, our seventeen-year-old, reports that a high school classmate lost her father.

And we learn at church that a fellow parishioner also died in the attack.

Part II – Aftermath

Almost overnight, following the attack on September 11th, the United States flag becomes omnipresent.

A transformation takes place, and wherever I look, there are the Stars and Stripes. It is as though, with one accord, Americans everywhere are reaching for a security blanket—of red, white, and blue.

From homes and on mailboxes, on buildings and barns, from highway overpasses, the nation's colors are being flown, painted, hung.

A groundswell is underway. Drivers and vehicles take part. Innumerable flags flap savagely up and down the highway, red and white stripes snapping fiercely at sixty-five miles per hour, from window mounts on cars and trucks.

Flag stickers appear in dollar stores. They can be affixed to notes, envelopes, folders. Along with other patrons, I purchase multiple packs.

The transformation is everywhere in evidence. I buy a bag of *M&M* candies, discovering only three colors inside—red, white, and blue.

It's days after the attack.

Commuting to work, another driver cuts sharply in front of me. Under normal circumstances, the experience might provoke a disparaging thought or comment on my part. Now, however, there is within me no animosity toward this fellow American. "He's not the enemy, Richard," I hear myself say.

The enemy struck on September 11th. Each of us was affected. Now we are all in this together.

Such is the sense of unity in the air. It is palpable—a feeling of oneness, a patriotic kinship unlike anything I've known.

I comment about this to my friend, Vic Ramsey. Vic is thirty years my senior and was twenty-one years old on another momentous day in U.S. history—June 6, 1944, D-Day. He has experienced this before.

"That's the way it was all during World War Two," he informs me.

It is four months later.

I'm in Jersey City, New Jersey, with fellow employees, for work-related training. Our accommodations are directly across the Hudson River from lower Manhattan and the former site of the World Trade Center.

"Let's visit *Ground Zero*," someone suggests.

A Wednesday evening expedition is organized.

Let us take a moment and examine a marvelous irony.

A youth grows up in the rural Midwest, in tranquil southeastern Wisconsin. His childhood is pleasant, and happy—but during these formative years, an irrational fear develops. It grows, and becomes a phobia.

What is the fear? What causes it, and why does it grow?

The impressionable youth experiences a nascent fear of big cities. It is induced by the daily news, and intensified over time by the shocking reports and recurring grim details therein of the cruel mayhem that big cities contain.

March 13, 1964. Queens, New York. Early morning.

A young woman, twenty-eight-year-old Catherine Susan Genovese— "Kitty" to her family and friends—is returning home to her apartment from her work as a sports bar manager.

She is attacked by Winston Moseley, a knife-wielding twenty-nine-year-old machine operator. He stabs her multiple times, and sexually assaults her. Kitty Genovese dies an hour later from her wounds.

The *New York Times* reports that thirty-eight witnesses living in the surrounding apartments hear Kitty Genovese scream for help, observe the attack, yet do nothing to save her. "I didn't want to get involved," says one of the witnesses, according to the *Times* article.

The Midwestern youth in Wisconsin is ten years old at the time of the sensational national news story.

July 13, 1966. Chicago, Illinois. 11:00 p.m.

Richard Franklin Speck, age twenty-four, breaks into a townhouse at 2319 East 100th Street.

The townhouse serves as a dormitory for eight student nurses who work at the South Chicago Community Hospital. At knifepoint, the eight are held captive by Speck in one of the bedrooms. During the next several hours, each is led out and, one by one, is assaulted, then strangled or stabbed to death.

There is one survivor—a ninth student nurse, Corazon

Amurao, who is spending the night. Amurao squeezes under a bed and hides while Speck is out of the room with one of his victims.

When the gruesome story breaks, it stuns the nation.

One may ask: How many times during one's formative years does the daily news include stories of murder, rape, robbery, assault, battery—violence of every kind?

How often is this reported as occurring in one of the various large cities of our nation?

And is this torrent tempered by equivalent illustrations of virtue—stories of kindness, gentleness, love?

If not, one might speculate: Can one grow up and, exposed to this ongoing barrage of negative news, *not* be affected, to some degree, as was the youth above?

Now then. You have surmised that I am the one portrayed, who grew up in the rural Midwest, in tranquil southeastern Wisconsin—with a phobia of big cities?

Very well. Let us continue.

September 11, 2001. New York City. Mid-morning.
Responding to the deadly terrorist attack and unprecedented emergency situation, and with black smoke billowing into the sky from above, hundreds of New York City rescue and emergency personnel, including firemen, police officers, paramedics, emergency medical technicians—some of whom are off duty, yet respond anyway—enter the burning twin towers of the crippled World Trade Center.

Forgoing their own safety, they search for office workers, provide assistance, and fight fires.

The situation deteriorates. Evacuation orders are issued.

Not all are able to evacuate in time. When the towers collapse, a total of 411 responders are still inside.

When I learn afterward of the 411, who, along with many others, perish when the towers collapse, a remarkable thing happens—my lifelong phobia dissipates completely.

It simply vanishes, so struck am I by the selfless dedication and sacrifice of the New York City rescue and emergency professionals.

And therein is the marvelous irony.

Consider: The nineteen terrorists of September 11 plot, prepare for, and carry out a coordinated, multitarget, lethal suicide attack. Among their objectives: the instilling of widespread fear.

Yet, regarding my fear—that which I have experienced for decades, that which I've known for so long—there occurs a completely opposite result.

So on January 9, 2002, class and workday over, and with dusk settling, I join my fellow employees for what becomes a somber pilgrimage into the wounded city.

Part III – The Wounded City

A commercial ferry transports us across the Hudson River to lower Manhattan.

Upon disembarking, we are within walking distance of the former site of the World Trade Center.

It is after dark.

With the street lamps and neon signs and brightly lit buildings of Manhattan illuminating the sidewalks along our way, and with sounds of nighttime traffic in the air, we journey several blocks on foot.

Then, as we approach *Ground Zero*, traffic subsides and we leave buildings and bright lights behind as we come upon a vast area of dark emptiness.

Separating us from this immense dark void, we encounter a tall chain link fence. And as we draw near, we see that the fence is blanketed by an incongruous, diverse array.

It is a great patchwork, a weather-worn profusion from around the country and beyond—the expression of an outpouring of support.

There are wreaths, flowers, letters, poems, posters, photographs, stuffed animals, foreign flags—and most numerous, US flags, in varied sizes, large and small.

The sentiment we observe expressed is apparent.

From a North Carolina community college there is a large canvas of white displaying the Stars and Stripes and in bold, black letters, the words **"United We Stand."** The canvas is covered with signatures in red and blue.
A German couple has sent an American flag. On the white stripes is a neatly hand-printed message: *"God bless. All sympathy from Germany. Corinna and Karl."*
From a middle school in Wisconsin there is a red, white, and blue poster with an enlarged, overhead snapshot of an outdoor gathering of the student body. They are standing together to form the letters **"USA."**

Our pilgrimage ends at an observation platform. There we quietly join a small gathering of other late-day visitors.

There is little to see at this hour.
In the distance are floodlights, scattered like stars across a night sky. They illuminate work areas. Muted sounds of heavy machinery can be heard—part of the around-the-clock clearing and removal operation underway since the attack.

On the platform, the atmosphere is solemn. Conversations are in undertones.

I monitor the time. It is just after 9:00 p.m. At 9:11, I snap a photo of the distant lights.
In the assemblage we meet Ana, a New York City employee who speaks with a foreign accent.
Ana works at the South Street Seaport, which, we learn, is nearby. She was on her way to work on the day of the attack.

Ana shares with us an eyewitness account of the morning of September 11th.

From the Number Seven Queens train, Ana states, she saw the fireball of the second airliner impacting the tower.

Walking along Church Street, passing the World Trade Center, she paused when she saw bodies falling. When she could no longer bear to watch, she continued on.

Minutes later, the first tower collapsed.

She saw a huge cloud of dust and debris coming toward her. She ran for her life, as did the pedestrians around her.

She was knocked down by a man running by. With an apology, he stopped briefly, helped her to her feet, and they ran for cover.

We take the ferry back to Jersey City.

At our hotel, we chat with Elecia, on duty at the Front Desk. Elecia tells us that her mother was in the World Trade Center at the time of the attack.

She was on the eleventh floor, Elecia says, and evacuated safely.

Part IV – Conclusion

The months are passing. Things are returning to normal.

The groundswell is subsiding, the transformation winding down. The Stars and Stripes are no longer omnipresent at home and on the highway.

I see a flag one day lying unclaimed along the side of the road. I pull over, stop, and retrieve it, and the window mount to which it is attached.

Sometime later, rummaging through a storage box at home, I find a long-buried packet of slides.

I pause to view them, holding each one up to the light. They are snapshots of the Statue of Liberty, taken during a visit with Marcy to Liberty Island in New York Harbor in July of 1981.

I come across an image on one of the slides that causes me to stop and peer closer. And I make a surprising discovery.

The image I see, which I later enlarge and frame, occurred as our shuttle boat was departing Liberty Island and beginning its return to Battery Park. I took the picture as we were pulling away from shore.

The scene is a beautiful summer day, with blue sky, sunshine, and white clouds drifting.

In the left foreground looms the Statue of Liberty—tall, bold, with torch held high.

Captured in the center background, and seemingly dwarfed by Lady Liberty, who stands ever steadfast, ever calm and resolute, appear the World Trade Center twin towers.

Thought:
"The price of liberty
is eternal vigilance."
Thomas Jefferson

"If we simply and objectively consider the words of the Preamble, with attention to the phrase "and our Posterity," *is it not entirely evident that our Constitution pertains to* all Americans, *including the unborn?"*

—From **"We the People"**

We the People
and our Posterity
2013

Is it not true that the word "unalienable" means "inviolable," and "is not to be taken away"?

Introduction

The good news: Abortionist Kermit Gosnell's thirty-year practice has ended. Children will have the opportunity to be born and breathe and cry and eat and sleep and grow, who otherwise may have been denied their "unalienable" right to life.

The bad news: To what degree is each of us also guilty of the carnage that occurred in his "house of horrors" during those thirty years? And has occurred throughout the United States since 1973? And continues daily, with our full knowledge and tacit consent? With 56 *million* of America's posterity aborted since *Roe v. Wade?*

In this modern day, can anyone really claim not to be aware that life begins at conception?

And is not the federal *Life at Conception Act* precisely what is needed to protect the most vulnerable among us, and thus reaffirm and safeguard, once and for all, our God-given, premier *unalienable right to life*?

Background*

On Monday, Dr. Kermit Gosnell, 72, was convicted of first-degree murder in the deaths of three babies delivered alive at his abortion clinic in Philadelphia, Pennsylvania. Gosnell was also found guilty of involuntary manslaughter in the overdose death of an abortion patient. He was cleared in the death of a fourth baby.

Gosnell was also convicted of infanticide, racketeering and more than 200 counts of violating state abortion laws by performing third-term abortions or failing to counsel women 24 hours in advance.

In addition, his co-defendant, former clinic employee Eileen O'Neill, was convicted of taking part in a corrupt organization and illegally billing for her services as if she were a licensed doctor.

Also, four former clinic employees pleaded guilty to murder and four more to other charges. They included Gosnell's wife, Pearl, a cosmetologist who helped perform abortions.

Former clinic employees testified that Gosnell routinely performed illegal abortions past Pennsylvania's 24-week limit, that he delivered babies that were moving, breathing, or whimpering, and that he and his assistants dispatched the newborns by "snipping" their spines, as he referred to it.

The details came out more than two years ago during an investigation of prescription drug trafficking at Gosnell's clinic. Investigators said it was a foul-smelling "house of horrors" with bags and bottles of fetuses, including jars of severed feet, along with bloodstained furniture, dirty medical instruments, and roaming cats.

Pennsylvania authorities had not conducted routine

inspections of its abortion clinics for 15 years prior to the raid on Gosnell's facility. As a result, two top state health officials were fired, and Pennsylvania imposed tougher rules for clinics.

Gosnell did not testify, and his lawyer, Jack McMahon, called no witnesses in his defense. McMahon said it was "a very difficult case" to defend.

Gosnell portrayed himself as an advocate for poor and desperate women in an impoverished West Philadelphia neighborhood. He performed thousands of abortions over a thirty-year career, some on patients as young as 13. Authorities said the practice netted him approximately $1.8 million a year.

*By Maryclaire Dale of the Associated Press, in the *Washington Post Express* and *Washington Examiner* newspapers, Tuesday, May 14, 2013.

Discussion

Let us consider our United States Constitution, acknowledged to be and upheld as our supreme law of the land. And let us look at the Preamble to our Constitution:

"We the People of the United States, in Order to form a more perfect Union, establish Justice, insure domestic Tranquility, provide for the common defence, promote the general Welfare, and secure the Blessings of Liberty to ourselves and our Posterity, do ordain and establish this Constitution for the United States of America."

Dictionary.com defines *"posterity"* as *"succeeding or future generations collectively."*

Let us make what appears to be an obvious observation.

By ordaining and establishing our Constitution and including in the Preamble the phrase *"and our Posterity,"* did not the Framers clearly intend that the document's security and protection be extended not only to Americans alive at that time, but to all who would follow as well? All who were yet unborn? You, me, every one of us, of each present and future generation?

Could the intent be any clearer? Do the words not mean exactly what is indicated?

Must we not then ask ourselves: Is not the killing of those in the womb clearly in opposition to that which was intended by our Founders?

Shall we not then also ask ourselves: Is not the entire abortion "debate" irrelevant? That is to say, what is there to debate, or to argue? If we simply and objectively consider the words of the Preamble, with attention to the phrase, *"and our Posterity,"* is it not entirely evident that our Constitution pertains to *all* Americans, *including* the unborn?

Thought:
"The thief cometh not,
but for to kill, and to steal, and to destroy:"
John 10:10 [KJV]

The National Archives, Washington, DC
In the Rotunda of the National Archives, one can lean over the glass display
and be face-to-face with our original US Constitution.

George Washington

Mount Vernon

James Madison, seated; Dolly Madison

Montpelier

Thomas Jefferson

Monticello

Group III

Experience and Perspective

"If I could go back and speak with the person I was those many years ago, what would I say? What had been learned over the years that I would feel compelled to pass along? What observations could I make? What message could I share?"

—From **"A Journey in Time"**

A Journey in Time
2012

If you could meet the person you were forty years ago, what would you say to that person?

Prologue

The year is 1970. I'm seventeen, at home with my mother in the kitchen. We are engaged in a quiet conversation—discussing life, and the learning of lessons along the way. Mom is at the sink, in an unusually reflective mood, gazing out the window.

At seventeen, my adolescent world is relatively small, my teenage perspective limited.

Mom, on the other hand, has experienced much more than I, including the Great Depression and World War II. Her adult world is a great mystery to me, and her frame of reference, as a grownup, is far different from mine.

So I am all at once intrigued, and the tone of the conversation shifts abruptly, when my mother softly exclaims, "If I only knew then what I know now!"

It's a rare moment, and an unusual opportunity. It's as though the door to adulthood is creaking open, and I'm about to get a peek.

What does Mom know now, that she wishes she knew before?
What lessons have been learned? What wisdom acquired?

What special knowledge has been gained, and what unique insights realized, in the mysterious world that she, Dad, and their peers live in, called adulthood?

I am all ears—raptly attentive and eager for answers.

I learn no secrets, however.

Although I press—"What is it you know, Mom? Tell me!"—Mom finds herself unexpectedly at a loss for words.

The moment passes.

The conversation winds down.

And the door creaks shut.

Part 1

The postcard arrived in February:

> Mark your calendar!
> CLASS OF 1971
> 40 Year Reunion
> September 10th, 2011

Walking up the sidewalk with the mail, unmindful of all but the post card, and only vaguely aware of the late afternoon sunshine and semiwintry Virginia temperature, I was lost in thought.
Forty years.

That evening I placed the announcement on display at my bedside.
From time to time, during the ensuing months, I pondered the journey home.

September arrived.
I went online and booked a flight, then made a reservation with a Wisconsin bed-and-breakfast.
Soon after, as the date drew near, Marcy and I flew to Milwaukee and rented a car. We attended the reunion, which was the following evening. It was held at a supper club near my hometown.

The club was crowded, and noisy. Despite the clamor, I was happy to be in attendance.
There was dinner, music and dancing, and mingling throughout.

For three hours or so, with Marcy alongside, I encountered classmates who, four decades earlier, had been an integral part of my life, just as, likewise, I had been an integral part of theirs. As had occurred during the two previous reunions I attended, at twenty and thirty years, I was transported back in time, to a younger self, experiencing thoughts and impressions and memories that were still there, still part of me, after all the intervening years.

During our quiet drive afterward through the tranquil night, I reflected on the years gone by and all that had occurred since graduation day in June of 1971.

Thoughts and musings presented themselves:

If I could go back and speak with the person I was those many years ago, what would I say? What had been learned over the years that I would feel compelled to pass along? What observations could I make? What message could I share?

There were further musings:

During an encounter with my younger self, what would that person say to me? Would there be questions asked? If so, what would they be?

And another intriguing thought:

How would such an encounter occur?

These introspections occupied my mind as Marcy napped peacefully beside me and, road and midnight hour to ourselves, we traversed the quiet countryside of southern Wisconsin on our way back to our B & B.

Part 2

There wasn't a vehicle in sight.
 The young hitchhiker was experiencing an unintended solitude as he trudged the shoulder with his burdensome backpack and surveyed the seemingly interminable stretch of hill and highway descending before him.
 He was in the Cascade Range, in northern California, an hour or so outside of Redding, surrounded by a vast and rugged countryside of rocks and boulders and lonely, craggy terrain.
 The weather was fair, with sunshine, blue sky, and an occasional cloud drifting. That was in his favor.
 The remoteness of his travel route, however, had brought his forward progress to all but a standstill.

 He had been planning the journey, gathering the gear he would need, and preparing, for months.
 It would be an adventure—hitchhike west for the summer and see America. Apart from the rides he would rely upon, he would camp and cook and be self-sufficient.
 And, some weeks earlier, soon after his high school graduation, the adventure had begun.

 From his home in southeastern Wisconsin he had made his way northwest into Minnesota, into the Dakotas, across to Wyoming. He had pushed northward into Montana, westward to Idaho and Oregon, and finally south at the Pacific to California.

 The rides had been good, and until the present moment, he had considered the spirited undertaking a success, on several counts.

First, he had met an interesting cross section of individuals, on the road and along the way. Also, he had developed proficiency in the use of his camping and cooking gear. In this regard, he had achieved a desired degree of self-reliance, while expanding his horizons.

And, most notably, he had begun to see America.

In the Black Hills he had visited Mount Rushmore. In Wyoming he stopped at Devil's Tower. He saw his first bald eagle while skirting Yellowstone. He experienced Big Sky Country in Montana, and crossed the Rocky Mountains through the Lolo Pass into Idaho.

On a sunny afternoon in the desert of eastern Oregon, after being dropped off amid hundreds of square miles and innumerable acres of the region's indigenous sagebrush, he watched his ride turn from the highway onto a dirt trail leading to a ranch somewhere beyond the horizon. The vehicle grew ever smaller in the distance until it finally crested a hill and disappeared from view.

In the stillness that followed, with no other traffic on the road, afternoon became evening, evening turned to dusk, and night fell.

He camped adjacent to the highway.

During the long, quiet night amidst the vast acreage of green, aromatic sagebrush, the singularly sweet, pervasive smell impressed itself indelibly into his memory.

When he reached the forested Oregon coast, he took in the vista of the Pacific Ocean, turned southward to California, and camped among the giant conifers of Redwood National Forest. Heading inland from there, the white-capped symmetry of Mount Shasta soon came into view.

Which had all brought him to his current coordinates, north of Redding, trudging the shoulder of scenic, deserted US Highway 97, in the wilderness of the Cascades.

With the loss of momentum, the adventure had become an ordeal, and he had become an adventurer turned pack mule, burdened with tarp and sleeping bag and Sterno stove and canned heat and cookware and utensils and canteen and camp saw and hatchet and hunting knife and whetstone and waterproof matches and First Aid kit and food supplies and clothing and all that was required for self-sufficiency.

He was finding himself thoroughly uncomfortable as he trudged along.

His muscles ached under the load of the backpack. In addition, the nylon straps, despite their padding, squeezed his shoulders unrelentingly. The constant pressure and its adverse effect on circulation were causing tingling and numbness in his arms.

He tried periodically shifting the weight in an attempt to restore blood flow. The effort was partially successful, but short-lived.

Causing further discomfort, with each stride the aluminum frame prodded and pressed his torso and hips.

As for the sweltering he could feel in the small of his back, and the warm dampness there of his terry polo, there was but one remedy.

He stopped and released the pack. Maneuvering the burden from his shoulders, he swung the load to the ground.

The effect was immediate. Unburdened, he was free.

He stood, pack mule no longer, taking deep, leisurely breaths, enjoying the respite.

Languidly stretching and twisting, he slowly worked his shoulders and back. As he did so, he could feel his discomfort lessening, the tingling in his arms subsiding.

With his body recovering, he closed his eyes and, retreating within, relaxed and surrendered to the experience of the moment, inwardly exploring the sensations of his other senses—the unevenness of the gravel under his boots; the freshness of the air and the organic, outdoor mixture of scents; the warmth of the sunshine on his face; the rush of a sudden breeze through nearby pines, and then the gentle feel of it against his skin.

In his mind's eye he pictured the deserted highway. Instinctively he inclined an ear for the sound of a potential ride.

There was only the caw of a distant crow.

Part 3

"*You made a promise to yourself, didn't you?*"

The voice completely startled him. His eyes shot open. Was he imagining? No, he definitely heard someone speak.

"*I said, you made a promise to yourself, didn't you?*"

A short distance away, in the shadow of a giant boulder, stood a stranger near a large, flat rock.

What on earth ...? The young hitchhiker was certain he had been completely alone on the highway.

"*Where in the world did he come from?*" he thought to himself, bewildered.

Suddenly hopeful that the stranger might be his next ride, he looked around for a vehicle.

There was none.

"*Do you have a few moments?*"

The stranger was of average height and medium build. He was dressed casually, in khaki trousers, with a light khaki cardigan over a black collared shirt. His voice was relaxed, his tone friendly and inviting.

"*The next time I travel cross-country, I'm going to have my own set of wheels.*"

The young hitchhiker was confused.

"*I beg your pardon?*" He approached the boulder, leaving the backpack where it was.

"*That's the promise you made.*" The stranger gestured toward the highway. "*You were fantasizing about coasting down the mountain.*" The stranger smiled. "*And,*" he continued, "*you promised yourself that the next time you travel cross country, it'll be with wheels."*

The young hitchhiker was taken aback. It was what he had been thinking, just before he had stopped to rest.

The young hitchhiker's mind was racing.

Who is this person? What is he doing here? Why no vehicle?

He stopped at the huge boulder.

"Excuse me," he said, "but how in the world did you know what I was thinking back there?"

The stranger stood, calmly looking at the young hitchhiker. Finally, he spoke.

"Well," he said, his tone cordial, "this may not entirely answer your question, but forty years ago, on this same stretch of highway, during an adventure just like yours, I had the very same thought."

Part 4

*T*he highway remained deserted as the sun slowly arced its way across the afternoon sky.

An occasional squirrel or chipmunk appeared, darted about and was gone.

High above, a lone hawk circled.

The backpack, unmoved, stood like a sentinel at the side of the road, its shadow growing easterly on the surrounding gravel.

The stranger, meanwhile, and the young hitchhiker, were sitting on the large, flat rock. The stranger was speaking.

"Let me ask you something—hypothetically," the stranger was saying.

"Suppose," he continued, "that, years from now—after you get married, raise a family, have a career—you could return here, to this time and place, and meet the person you are now. Suppose the two of you could sit and talk and spend time together. Just suppose. What do you think that would be like?"

The young hitchhiker considered the curious question. As he thought about it, he wasn't sure what to say.

"Well," he began, searching for words, "I suppose if that were to happen, if I were to meet my future self..." His voice trailed off.

The young hitchhiker knew that such a thing was impossible and would never happen.

Still, something in the stranger's manner, something in how he asked the question, caused him to speculate.

"I suppose," he replied, "in a situation like that, I would want to ask questions."

Conclusion

"*S*o, how much do you want for it?"

The college student—he would soon be starting his first semester at the local community campus—was ready to close the deal.

"I've got an offer for sixty dollars."

The student had already decided. He needed wheels, the yellow Schwinn was almost brand new, and with the booming popularity of ten-speed bicycles, he felt fortunate to have found this one.

"I'll give you sixty-five," he said.

*T*here was hardly a cloud in the sky.

Classes were over, the weekend was beginning, and autumn in southeastern Wisconsin offered days on end of sunshine and cool, fresh air.

What he enjoyed most about the bicycle—besides the fall foliage, the endorphin high, and the freedom of the open road, the student decided—was the solitude.

The hours in the saddle, alone with his thoughts, were an opportunity to reflect, ponder, meditate.

During these times of quiet introspection, the student's thoughts often turned to an unusual encounter of some months previously. The encounter had occurred during a summer hitchhiking adventure out West.

"Suppose," a stranger had said to him, on a deserted stretch of wilderness highway in northern California, "that, years from now—after you get married, raise a family, have a career—you could return here, to this time and place, and meet the person you are now. Suppose the two of you could sit and talk and spend time together. What do you think that would be like?"

"I suppose," he had replied, "in a situation like that, I would want to ask questions."

"What kind of questions?" the stranger had asked.

Several had come immediately to mind: Who am I going to marry? What is my wife like? Are we happy? How many children do we have?

Surprisingly, the stranger had brushed his questions aside.

"Never mind that," the stranger had said. "That will all happen naturally.

"Listen carefully," he then said. "If you were to meet your future self, this is what he would say to you. This is what he *would want you to know.*

"First, life is all about making choices. And we don't always choose wisely.

"Secondly, life plays for keeps. There is no going back to change the past, no matter how much we wish it could be otherwise.

"Thirdly, we're human, which means we're fallible. We make mistakes, and we must learn to accept that.

"And lastly, mistakes are not final. But getting back on track may take time. So it's important to hang in there, no matter what."

"How do you know that's what my future self would say to me?" the student had asked.
The stranger had simply looked at him.
"I'll tell you what," he said. "Remember this moment, remember what I've told you, and in forty years, you decide if I was right."

Thought:
"So, Mom—would you agree?"

Group IV

The Spirit of Adventure

"One night, well after dark, after I had set up camp in the grove, I was enjoying a solitude at the beach. The air was warm and the night was still, with a gentle surf. There was a full moon just beginning to rise over the ocean. The water sparkled from the full moon. It was a beautiful moment—and so peaceful."

—From **"A Florida Adventure"**

A Florida Adventure
2018

If, at age nineteen, in December, you were to ride your ten-speed bicycle from Wisconsin to Florida, then spend the better part of three months camping and visiting beaches from Pensacola to Key West—what do you think that would be like?

Prologue

She was, quite simply, the most captivating creature he had ever encountered. And he was finding himself utterly enchanted. In a word, he was moonstruck. And his life would never be the same.

It was August of 1972. He was nineteen years old, in college. Enjoying a relatively carefree summer lifestyle, he had packed a swimsuit and towel and had pedaled his ten-speed bicycle from his home in southeastern Wisconsin to nearby Silver Lake—a popular, pleasant retreat of Mother Nature's, typical of the region.

His destination—the grassy beach and designated swimming area there—was the same as each of the frequent and previous sunny summer afternoons. And, as on these other days, he had, after a while, ventured into the deeper water, swimming across the section of lake to a distant wooden pier that jutted out. And, as before, he had climbed onto the pier, availing himself of a wooden bench there.

His intention was unchanged—to rest a moment, leisurely

enjoying a brief solitude and the warmth of the sunshine on his face—before diving back into the water and returning to the beach.

On this day, however, his solitude ended unexpectedly with the approach of an aluminum canoe. And as the canoe drew near, he observed two female occupants in bathing suits—one approximately his age, the other younger. It was apparent they were about to dock at his pier.

"Ship, ahoy," he called out, in a friendly voice, then mentally edited his remark. It's not a ship, he thought to himself, it's a canoe.

The occupants pulled alongside, stowed their paddles, and climbed onto the pier. As they did so, he engaged the elder of the two in polite conversation—upon which she proceeded to join him at the bench.

Her name was Diana. She was sixteen years old, he learned, from the Caribbean island of Grenada, in the West Indies. She and her younger sister—her companion in the canoe—along with their parents and her younger brother, were on vacation, visiting her grandparents there at the lake. Her grandparents owned the pier, and the wooden bench on which they sat, as well as the year-round, lakeside cottage nearby. Her mother and father, originally from Milwaukee, had a glass-bottom boat business in Grenada, where she had been born, and where they lived.

As the conversation continued and the moment unfolded, he became intrigued. This was a girl unlike any he had met heretofore—a visitor from an exotic, faraway island paradise, who spoke with a soft, curiously melodic accent.

She was 67 inches and 112 pounds of God's finest craftsmanship. She had a lovely countenance, with intelligent eyes and a warm, winsome smile. She had apparently been swimming earlier. Her shoulder length, sandy-colored hair was not yet dry.

She was gracious in her manner, with an easy, relaxed charm. Most notably, and which he could not help but observe, she was a slender reed of a girl, with flawless skin and toned, adolescent curves, which, in her scant bikini, were unabashedly on display, there in the sunshine on the pier.

Upon explaining his presence—that he had come across the lake from the distant swimming area—she commented, *"That's quite a swim."* He shrugged it off. He had been on the swim team in high school. He didn't consider his venture across the small parcel of lake noteworthy to any degree.

When he mentioned during their conversation that, among other things, he enjoyed bowling, she spoke up and said she had always wanted to do that. So he offered to take her bowling that evening.

After returning home and preparing for the evening ahead, he borrowed the family car and returned later to the cottage for their date. Upon meeting her mother and father, and agreeing on a curfew, she was entrusted into his care. He escorted her to the local bowling alley and introduced her to the game.

During the following days they took walks together at the lake—sometimes hand-in-hand—until her family's vacation drew to a close. He asked then if he might write to her—she was to attend high school in Fort Lauderdale, Florida—and she responded in the affirmative.

As the summer ended and another semester at the local community campus began, he did write to her, as he had said he would, and she wrote back. As the semester progressed, he realized he had to see her again.

With his realization, and subsequent resolve, he took some moments to consider his options.

Driving to Florida was out of the question—he had no vehicle, nor could he borrow or rent one.

Hitchhiking, he decided, was also not going to be an option. He had already done that, having thumbed his way West the previous summer, after graduation from high school, with a backpack, to see America. He had promised himself during an unanticipated lull in that trip that the next time he traveled cross-country, it would be with his own set of wheels.

As he pondered his dilemma, the solution presented itself.

He could ... ride his bicycle. To Florida. To Fort Lauderdale. To see her again.

He considered the option. For the past year, ever since returning from his hitchhiking trip out West, and shortly thereafter procuring his first ten-speed bicycle, and then, some months later, upgrading to his current, higher performance Schwinn, he had all but lived on the bike. He pedaled every day to school and back. And each day to his part-time job. And, when he wasn't at school, or at work, or at home studying, he would be out riding, for hours at a time, experiencing the scenic back roads and byways of *The Badger State*, for the sheer joy and exhilaration of it.

Yes, he decided—he could indeed ride his bicycle. All the way to Florida. And, furthermore, he would make a grand adventure out of it. Not only would the trip include pedaling to Fort Lauderdale, but it would encompass the remainder of the winter, and he would take in as much as he could of what *The Sunshine State* had to offer.

When he presented his plan to his parents, his father thoughtfully responded with a remark that, years later, he would decide was the wisest thing any father could say to his son, given the circumstances: *"Well, if that's what you want to do, then now is the time to do it. Otherwise, later on, you'll always wish you had."*

Next, he arranged with his employer to take the rest of the winter off—with his job awaiting him upon his return in the Spring.

Then, he gathered his gear and readied his bicycle.

With his plans in order, the only thing delaying his departure was school. And in that regard, unlike his first two semesters the previous year, when he had taken a full load of credits, this Fall semester he had opted to register for only one class—a Sociology course entitled *"Marriage and the Family."* The final exam was on December 18th.

On December 19th, at dawn, having adequately prepared for the journey, he dressed warmly and wheeled his gear-laden bicycle out of the garage and into the frigid Wisconsin morning.

With a final goodbye to his family, he flung his leg over the saddle and, ignoring the snow and cold, settled in for a long day's ride—with a vision of palm trees and warm sand and ocean surf in his head.

Part 1
Arrival

Friday, December 29, 1972

Dear Mom, Dad, and brothers,
To begin with, the trip down, as I mentioned on the phone, was mostly drudgery. The scenery was pretty much the same almost all the way. To recap, let me summarize as follows:

I left with it overcast and it remained so all the way to Meridian, Mississippi. I sure was looking forward to sunshine. I encountered fog the first few days, some of it quite heavy, and there was light mist, but then the roads dried up. After I got south of Decatur, Illinois, there wasn't any more snow. Then it was dull brown until Meridian.

My route was as follows: I took Wisconsin Highway 83, primarily, until I got into Illinois—which was about six p.m. that first day. Then I took Illinois Highway 47 to Decatur, where I picked up U.S. Highway 51. Following 51 took me into Kentucky. Then U.S. Highway 45 took me through Tennessee and Mississippi to Mobile, Alabama. I skirted the city and took U.S. Highway 90 east into Florida.

I traveled all different hours, and no two of my days so far have been the same. Sometimes I pedaled all day and into the night, until 1 or 2 a.m. Then I would continue around noon. Or if I called it quits early at dusk, I'd be back on the road at 9 or 10 the next morning.

All in all, I found the best riding was at night, when there was no wind and very few cars.

I've been eating at various places, from grocery stores to Holiday Inns. I've spent nine nights in motels, with an average cost of about $5 a night.

I got into Florida yesterday around noon, passed through the hustle and bustle of Pensacola City, and then arrived at Fort Pickens State Park, where I am now, waiting for the sun to peek over the horizon after spending my first night under the stars.

To get back to the scenery en route: I've had sunshine since Meridian, Mississippi. The landscape is green, and the 30- and 40-degree temperatures I experienced all the way down have been replaced with what is comparable to balmy Spring days in Wisconsin. When I got into Pensacola yesterday afternoon, it was 70 degrees. The low last night must have been in the 40's. I was nice and toasty in my sleeping bag.

It's warmer than usual. According to a fellow I talked to last night and again just now, this is the nicest day so far. He says it's usually freezing at this time in the morning, but it must be in the 50's.

The only difficulty I've had is pain in my knees. The first day it was just my right knee, then both. I think it's due to the pressure and rubbing of my pants. It's better since I no longer need my long thermal underwear. It's bothersome, but I can walk. (Hobble would be a better word.) The worst is over now, so here's hoping the more leisurely pace and warmer weather will help.

My plan is to continue along the Gulf, traveling however things work out. I want to find a spot where I can stay for a while, so you can send a few things I now can use. If you would like to get them ready, I'll advise when and where to send them.

I'll be mailing some things home, and if you would prepare the following to send to me, I'd appreciate it. I'll trade my tan sport shoes for the hiking boots I've worn thus far. Also, please send my light blue jeans from my closet. And from my drawer in the dresser please send my light blue shorts, and my striped polo shirt with the V-neck zipper. That should be all the clothes I need other than what I have.

There is another thing I would like, though, that I meant to bring. In the middle drawer of the vanity is an envelope from the Schwinn Company. In the envelope is a booklet on the care of one's bicycle. Please add it to my package. Then, all bills of mine—such as postage, and the cost of dry cleaning my jacket when I send it back, and the dollar I owe for my bicycle insurance policy—will be reimbursed when I return.

I mentioned on the phone something that happened on December 24th, in Selmer, Tennessee. I was pedaling up a long hill when a car passed me and pulled off to the side of the road. The driver called me over and introduced himself as James Whirley. He said he and his family had seen me riding through town earlier, when they went to church. They thought it would be nice to invite me to dinner. (This was around noon.) I accepted, then followed him back up the road and met his family. He has a lovely wife and daughter, two energetic young sons, and an infant son.

Well, I sure had a feast. There was turkey, dressing,

giblets and gravy, pumpkin bread, corn, beans, cranberry sauce, and rolls, and although I had eaten a small restaurant breakfast earlier, I just ate and ate, and finally couldn't eat another bite. It was delicious.

His brother-in-law and sister came over during the meal. His brother-in-law was the picture of the fine Southern gentleman, tall, and dressed to perfection in a beautiful blue suit. When we were introduced, he commented in a Southern drawl, *"You sound like a Yankee."*

Well, I'm getting hungry, and I have ten miles to peddle to the supermarket and post office in Gulf Breeze, so I'm going to pack up and head out. For now, 'tis I, the Yankee, signing off. Love, Rick

P.S. So far, I've traveled about 1,050 miles.

Part 2
Gulf Breeze

Sunday, December 31, 1972

Dear Family,

I'm beginning to lose track of time, and I know once I'm lying on sunny beaches for days on end I will for sure, but before that happens, I'll recap the last couple of days for you.

I left off Friday morning, in Fort Pickens State Part, and was just about to pack up and head into Gulf Breeze. When I arrived in town, I picked up some postcards and prepared the package of things that I don't need anymore. By the time I had prepared the package and mailed it, along with my letter, it was around noon.

I stayed in the post office and settled down to sending out the handful of postcards I had picked up. I sent one to the James Whirley family in Tennessee, who I've introduced to you and to whom I promised to write. As I was sending these out, I got into a conversation with a lady who asked if that was my bike outside. After talking briefly, she invited me to their home. I'm writing from there now, where I've spent the last two nights.

They—Bob and Maxine Cameron, and their two daughters, Leslie and Susan, ages 14 and 13—just got back from an extended vacation, touring Europe and Africa. Bob is a doctor, and Maxine is a poetess. Leslie has a horse and is training it. They're very hospitable. Last night we went out to dinner. Their home is right on the Gulf of Mexico here in Pensacola Beach, and as I look out the window I can see the surf not a hundred yards away.

The weather hasn't been pleasant. It's warm (50 or 60 degrees) but has been overcast. It rained off and on yesterday, and quite a bit last night. I'm ready for more sunshine and hope to be able to continue soon. My next stop is Fort Walton Beach, thirty miles along the coast. There's a Gulfarium there I may visit (porpoises, exhibitions and such).

I hope to be able to stop for about a week, soon, so I can send for my things, and clean my bike. I don't think my back spokes will ever shine like they once did.

My knees are much better. When I ride it doesn't hurt. I've done a lot of relaxing (yesterday I hardly got outside) and I'm sure the rest has done me a world of good.

Bob and Maxine are watching a football game on TV, and the two girls just left for babysitting until the wee hours tomorrow morning. (It's around 3:30 in the afternoon.) It's drizzly outside, but I hope the sun finds me on my way tomorrow morning. I can't wait to get to where it's really warm. You can swim here if you want, and right now there are surfers in sight, but it's really not the season.

The Pensacola area is lovely. There are miles and miles of white, sandy beach. Maxine says it's part of Florida few people know about. There are palm trees, and inland, one can see Spanish moss in some areas. Picturesque, even without sunshine.

Well, 'til next time, whenever and wherever that will be. Love, Rick

Part 3
Fort Walton Beach

Friday, January 5, 1973
Early afternoon

Hello everybody,
Today is gorgeous. The sky is blue, and the temperature is a balmy 75 or 80 degrees. I'm writing from a cozy wayside east of Perry on Highway 27. I slept here last night, had a good breakfast as the sun came up, and have spent the rest of the morning cleaning my bike.

To bring you up to date, let me continue where I left off, on December 31st.

I spent the rest of the day at the Camerons' and had a quiet New Year's Eve with them. The two girls had gone babysitting, and later in the evening a friend, John, came over. We just relaxed. I went to bed around 10:30.

New Year's Day was overcast, but dry, and after a hearty breakfast, I was able to continue my journey. Bob was gone, but the girls and Maxine were there to see me off.

As it turned out, fifteen miles down the road, as I was passing the Navarre campground, it began to rain. I pulled in, took shelter, and waited.

Well, it rained off and on the rest of the afternoon. I reluctantly resigned myself to spending the night. It was chilly, and it continued wet and rainy all night, but I was okay. The next morning's sky was as dismal as ever, and the prediction of it being that way for the next thirty-six hours didn't brighten my spirits, but after a nice breakfast and shower, I felt better. I had planned on spending another night there, if not two, but lo and behold, towards noon the sky improved and the road dried up, and I was off.

On into Fort Walton Beach I went, with a sixty percent chance of rain, increasing to seventy percent by night. I had a good meal at a Ponderosa Steakhouse ($1.71), and visited the Gulfarium, catching the last show of the day at 4 p.m.

There were three attractions. First there were two porpoises doing stunts. Then there was a diver with large

turtles, stingrays, a sawfish, small sharks, and other fish. Then there were trained seals.

The weather was cool and overcast, threatening rain. A five o'clock dreary dark sky saw me on my way. I pedaled and pedaled, not wanting to be caught in the rain—through Panama City and the thick fog that had developed. At 4:30 Wednesday morning I was exhausted. I camped at a roadside park, just past Mexico Beach on U.S. Highway 98.

I woke up about 7 a.m., even though I had only slept two hours, and struggled against a headwind into Port St. Joe. I had breakfast, then stopped at the bank to inquire about a $10 Traveler's Check I lost in Tennessee. I got the number for the nearest American Express Office. I'll find out if there is one in Gainesville, where I'm headed now.

I struggled against a stiff headwind into Apalachicola. I

ate as dusk settled, then continued in the dark through thick fog, thankful for no more wind.

It was a pleasant ride to the roadside park two miles before Carrabelle. I stopped around 8:30 p.m. and got a good night's rest. I woke up thoroughly refreshed there yesterday morning, had a delicious breakfast in Carrabelle, then continued my leisurely pace. The weather yesterday morning was overcast and gray, but towards noon the overcast moved out to sea, bringing sunny blue skies.

It was unusually warm yesterday, reaching 80 degrees—a record for Florida in these parts, I learned. I pedaled along, enjoying the beautiful countryside and forest along U.S. Highway 319, picked up Highway 98 again, and continued toward Perry. Towards dusk I got a thirty-mile lift from two guys going into Perry. That's happened a few times along the way—being offered a lift. Once for 100 miles in Illinois, to outrun an ice storm, and shorter distances, five and seven miles, here and there as well.

I ate in Perry, leisurely rode here, and spent a very comfortable night, except for a few mosquitos. Earlier, a couple from Michigan stopped with a camper. They left me with my canteen full of water, and gave me a couple of oranges, too.

Well, enough for now. Time to finish cleaning my bike and move on—maybe after sunbathing.

For now, I bid thee a pleasant day. Rick

Part 4
High Springs

Sunday, January 14, 1973

Dear Family,

I'm finally savoring the sunshine. But before I get to that, let me recap. I left you at a wayside east of Perry, and was about to continue, after possibly sunbathing. Well, I did lie on my tarp in the sunshine, and it was great. I'm glad I grabbed that opportunity. Little did I know what lay ahead. I continued about eighteen miles to Mayo. There was a wayside park, and I decided to spend the night.

The next day was sunny and warm again. I got to High Springs and decided this was the place at which I could languish for a week while awaiting my things. The evening was cloudless, and I rode to O'Leno State Park near High Springs to spend the night. I got there after dark, and there were more stars out than ever before, it seemed. It was nice and warm, and soon I was comfortably in my sleeping bag under my tarp, looking forward to a week of sunshine.

I slept, then was awakened by a sudden, cold wind—which was followed by rain. It rained all night, off and on. Well, to make a long week short, I didn't see the sun at all while awaiting my package, and the temperature dropped steadily—accompanied by wet weather. It in the 30's and 40's. And so damp. It goes right through you. Friday the package arrived, and I lit out, with predictions of low 20's expected.

I got to Ocala Friday evening and stayed at the Salvation

Army Lodge, not wanting to brave the cold anymore. (I stayed at the S.A. Lodge in Gainesville too, and escaped a whole night of rain and cold.) Then yesterday morning the sky was cloudless, and I looked forward to my first sunrise in what seemed a long time. It was cool in the morning, but the sun warmed things up, with a high in the low 50's.

Last night it was cold again. I camped at a roadside park near here. When I got up this morning the water in my canteen was frozen, my bike had frost on it, and it wouldn't shift because it was frozen solid. I was okay. It's another clear, sunny day (two in a row!) and although it's only in the 50's, the sun is warm. I'm in Silver Springs in a little park, and I have my shirt off for only the second time so far. But there's a lot more ahead.

I bought a collapsible Sterno stove, and Canned Heat, and a Teflon skillet, and canvas saddlebags, and food, and now I'm completely independent for my meals. However, all my gear is too much to carry on the bike. So I'm going to buy a small bicycle trailer. Maybe the Ocala Bike Center has one.

Last Saturday I stopped there and had my rear wheel aligned. Also, two broken spokes were replaced. And I replaced my generator light. It had given me trouble off and on along the way, then stopped working altogether en route to Ocala.

Until next time, Rick.

Part 5
Ocala

Wednesday, January 17, 1973

Dear Family,
I'm east of Ocala, at a wayside fringing Ocala National Forest. I've just had lunch, consisting of two cheeseburgers with fried onions, along with coleslaw mixed with bananas and raisons, and Carnation Instant Milk. My little Sterno stove is a real gem.

The weather's been improving steadily. It's been sunny every day since last Saturday, and temperatures have risen. It's beautiful, as I sit here in my shorts and polo shirt.

I managed to pick up a Cannondale "Bugger" in Ocala, buying the only one in town. The Bugger is a small aluminum bicycle trailer, and as you can imagine, it's quite handy. I'm stocked up on supplies to last me several days, and to give you an idea of what I can carry, I'll list the food I have. I'm at peak carrying capacity.

I have eggs; bacon; ground beef; chicken; a Hunt's skillet Oriental meal; onion, mushroom and chicken gravy mixes; an onion; carrots; margarine; peanut butter; honey; olive oil; coleslaw; mixed salad; bananas; raisons; dry cereal; instant oatmeal; seasoning salt; Tang; Carnation Instant Milk; Spaghetti and Sloppy Joe seasoning mixes;
hamburger seasoning; cheese; instant cocoa mix; wieners; spaghetti; sea shell noodles; pumpernickel bread; Bisquick; instant potatoes; and a supply of Sterno Canned Heat. I'm just about a ten-speed supermarket. It's great! Well, time to do dishes and move on. Rick

Thursday, January 18, 1973

I'm twenty-six miles east of Ocala in the Juniper Springs Recreation Area, in the heart of the Ocala National Forest. The Recreation Area is centered around a spring from which flows 8½ million gallons of crystal clear, 72-degree water daily, year-round. I'm lying in the sunshine in my swimsuit next to the spring.

There's a circular pool built around the spring, and surrounding the pool is the picnic area, and with the palm trees, hardwoods, and Spanish moss and other exotic flora, it looks like a billionaire's backyard. I arrived just as the sun was about to set last evening (around 6). I struggled against a stiff headwind all afternoon, and with the load I was pulling, I was ready for a good meal and night's rest. I got both.

Today is the first day in my swimsuit. I've had my shirt off a couple of times already, and I'm starting to tan. I don't see a cloud anywhere. Love, Rick

Thursday, January 18, towards sunset

I'm still at Juniper Springs. I met an older gentleman from Wisconsin (Adams County), and he invited me to his campsite. His wife was killed in a car accident eleven years ago.

I went swimming, then snorkeling. The spring is about twenty feet deep.

I think I'll be leaving tomorrow morning. Say, I haven't mentioned it since my first two letters, but my knees are fine. The first day into Florida they seemed to heal overnight. Until next time, Rick

Friday, January 19, afternoon

Hello again,

Had a nice afternoon with Horace Guthrie, my companion of yesterday. He'll be eighty years old on my birthday, May 6. Real nice fellow. He gave me his address and showed me on a Wisconsin map where he lives.

Last night after dark I was sitting at our picnic table, enjoying the evening—watching the stars come out and the full moon rise and listening to the raccoons begin to move around. Horace was down by the pool watching some slides of Panama a fellow presented. It was quiet.

He left me a flashlight. It wasn't long before a raccoon came into our clearing and began to dig around in the ash pile about twenty feet from me. I shined the light on him, and he left. This happened several times. Later the same thing happened with an armadillo.

I continued my ride this morning and pedaled south to Dorr Lake Recreation Area. I'm back in my swimsuit, basking by a lovely blue lake among the pines, just off the road. The travel bug is biting (too much lying around). So I think I'll head out — to Tampa and Sarasota.
For now, Rick

Part 6
Lake Worth

Wednesday, January 31, 1973

Dear Family,
I'm on the East Coast now, in Barton Park, next to the blue Atlantic, in Lake Worth—seven miles south of Palm Beach and West Palm Beach. I'll be here a few days, cleaning and waxing my bike, and relaxing and getting a tan. I arrived here yesterday afternoon.

To bring you up to date since the Friday the travel bug bit (it seems so long ago—a lot has happened, and many miles have been traveled), I continued to Tampa, arriving Saturday afternoon. I didn't know how long I was going to stay, and as it turned out, I stayed all week, leaving last Friday.

I toured the city. I also pedaled to the Tampa International Jetport, a new and unique airport—*"designed to meet the challenge of the jet age."* It was impressive—so clean and fresh and efficient. Saw, up close, my first Boeing 747 Jumbo Jet.

Eager to be off, I hit the road Friday. I rode through Clearwater to the beach, glanced at the bikinis (longest glance I ever took), then headed south to Sarasota. I ended up at a little wayside.

I continued to Fort Myers, then rode east—with a tremendous tailwind. I stopped at a private campground for the night. I met some nice people—one person in particular.

Very interesting fellow. He calls himself *"Long Island Fred"*—from New York, of course. We played chess. He's almost seventy, plays the mandolin, paints, and looks like Ernest Hemingway.

I continued to West Palm Beach, then Palm Beach, then south along the coast to here.

About the Bugger—it's working out well. It took some getting used to, pulling all my gear, but after adjusting, I'm once again able to travel along at ten to fifteen miles per hour. Rick

Thursday, February 1, 1973

I cleaned my Bugger yesterday and gave it two coats of wax. I also started cleaning my bike.

I took a dip at dawn. Swimming in the ocean here is very different from a Wisconsin lake.

There is a constant and strong wind blowing off the water. The beach slopes steeply, with heavy surf. As you enter, the undertow nearly throws you off balance. When the next wave crashes, it almost knocks you over.

I've continued cleaning my bike. My front spokes are as shiny as ever.

For now, time for some pancakes. Rick

Monday, February 5, 1973

Dear Family,
It's approaching suppertime and sundown. I have mixed vegetables to heat up, and some turkey drumsticks. My bicycle is clean now. I'm still here at Barton Park, on the ocean near Lake Worth. Today has been beautiful—sunny and in the 80's. I have the beginning of a tan.

An interesting thing happened last Thursday evening. I had arrived Tuesday and had camped here Tuesday and Wednesday. I had asked the caretaker whether it was okay to pitch my tarp at night. He said it was okay, and that I shouldn't be bothered—and I wasn't, for two nights.

Then Thursday I was awakened by a flashlight in my eyes and a policeman, who informed me that there was a city ordinance against sleeping in the park. (Lake Worth being the city.) He told me I had to leave. There were motor homes in the parking lot, and he was ordering them away, too. Anyway, I had my bike taken apart (the wheels and generator light were off), having been cleaning it earlier. I reassembled it and pondered my next move.

It had rained off and on earlier, and it was about to rain again any minute. That, and trying to find a place at night, made me hesitant to depart. So I moved to a sheltered area next to the restrooms and snuggled down among the picnic tables to resume my night's rest.

Well, the policeman came back, and a second time I awoke to a flashlight in my eyes. Then he arrested me and charged me with "lounging." It rained hard for a few minutes, then stopped, leaving puddles all around. (It made me glad I didn't move on.) The policeman called a fellow officer over, and they frisked me, and then took me and all my gear to the station.

I was placed in a cell with another fellow (I could have had one by myself if I'd wanted) and relaxed for the night, glad to be out of the wet weather. Friday morning came,

along with breakfast, and I settled back to a relaxing morning, confident I'd be out in no time.

Shortly thereafter I was fingerprinted, and a mug shot was taken. Then back to the cell. Oh well, I thought, they'll be back for me before long. A janitor came by and gave us razors. Then the hallway was silent, with no one else passing by.

The morning began to drag. My cell mate, about seventy, who was arrested for "causing an accident," said he'd been taken to court the day after being arrested, early in the afternoon—so I figured someone would come for me soon. Well, nothing happened. The minutes became hours, and noon came and went. The afternoon dragged. I was grateful for four National Geographic magazines that my cell mate had. Otherwise, there was absolutely nothing to do.

I decided I wanted OUT. That, combined with the prospect of spending the weekend there, put me by suppertime in a state of controlled frenzy. I hadn't *asked* how long I'd be in or what lay ahead. And not knowing made me panicky.

Anyway, when the fellow brought the meals, I requested

to bail myself out, which I did, having all of $27 bail on my head, I discovered. And I learned that my court appearance would be Tuesday. I rode to a nearby park and campground (upon learning of it from the officer), but it was full, and people were being turned away. I went to a spot near the entrance and called it a day, rolling out my sleeping bag under a tree near a restroom. The stars were out, the night was warm, and the mosquitos were savage, being right next to a stream.

After a miserable rest battling mosquitos, a cold front passed through. The calm became windy, the stars disappeared, and it began to rain. (It had been raining earlier in the day, one thing which made me feel a *little* better as I looked out from my jail cell.) I was soon all wet, not having bothered to put up my tarp (it was sundown when I bailed myself out, and dark by the time I departed the police station) and I took shelter beneath an overhead section outside the washroom. I moved my wet, salty bike over (the salt had accumulated from Barton Park, with the wind carrying a mist off the ocean) and settled into a cold, damp sleeping bag.

I managed to sleep, and awoke to overcast sky and damp surroundings. I packed my wet things (Saturday morning), went to a shopping center and laundromat in town, and prepared to salvage the day. I washed and dried my clothes, and dried my tarp and sleeping bag, and started to feel better. A haircut helped as well.

The sun came out then, a welcome sight, and the rest of the day was nice. I went to a spaghetti supper, having seen the notice in the barbershop window. I found another camping spot—south on A1A about a quarter of a mile. It's secluded, in a thick grove of coconut palm trees, just past the hotels, and right next to the ocean. I've had two great

nights there, sleeping ever so well, and am looking forward to tonight.

Coconuts lie about, inside the grove around my camping spot. I've been husking and eating them—they're full of milk and white meat.

Well, I've had my drumsticks and vegetables. It's dark now, and time to ride to my camp site. My court appearance is tomorrow morning at 8:30 (I get my $27 back), and then I was going to continue south on A1A. But it's supposed to be nice now for a while so I may stick around. Love, Rick

Tuesday morning, February 6, 1973

P.S. I was fined $5.00, with $2.00 in court costs.

Postscript

Christmas Eve, 2018

Dear Family and Friends,
Well, it's good to be back at the keyboard, after a five-year hiatus. That is to say, this is the first **Christmas** Newsletter since 2013.

If interested, here is a summary of the remainder of the journey:

I continued south on A1A—visiting Delray Beach, Boca Raton, Pompano Beach, Lauderdale by the Sea—biking, camping, and spending day after day in the fresh air and sunshine—swimming, bodysurfing, sunbathing. The sound of the surf became my daily companion. I remember times when, after a night of camping, I was the first to arrive at the beach in the morning—and then, after a long day in the sun, with people coming and going all day, I was the last to depart in the evening, as well.

I preferred the grassy areas, settling in for the day. I would lay out my 7 x 8-foot canvas tarp; then inflate my air mattress and place it on the tarp; then roll out my sleeping bag on the air mattress—and cover both with a white sheet that I would tuck in, and on which I would lie. I used Johnson's Baby Oil to tan, as did most serious sunbathers at that time.

When I got to Fort Lauderdale, I made my way to Pine Crest School, at 1501 NE 62nd Street, and inquired at the office regarding a certain young lady enrolled there. The receptionist was courteous and helpful. I waited outside in the sunshine, and there she was, walking back from class. Diana almost didn't recognize me. The first words out of her mouth were, *"You're so brown!"* And I was.

I biked through Homestead and spent time in the Everglades—where I met up with *Long Island Fred* again, at Grossman Hammock State Park. We played more chess. There was a pond, and a tiny beach. Out in the water were alligators, lying at the surface. They didn't bother bathers.

After the Everglades, I continued on U.S. Route 1 through the Florida Keys, biking mostly at night, after traffic subsided. Did you know there is a bridge in the Keys that is *seven miles long*? It's called, appropriately, **Seven Mile Bridge**. If you ride across it on a bicycle during the night when there is no traffic, and you stop in the middle, with miles in either direction, it's totally dark and peaceful, all ocean and quiet night sky—and stars all the way to the horizon.

If you come visit us in Northern Virginia and stay in our guest room, which you are welcome to do anytime, many of the sea shells in the dry aquarium in the guest room came from that ride through the Keys.

I arrived in Key West on Friday, March 2, 1973.

I remember having lunch in an RV park, on a picnic table in the sunshine. All was quiet, and the moment was peaceful. Then, from one the recreational vehicles, wafted a Nat King Cole song, *"**Mona Lisa**."* Every time I hear the song, it takes me back to that sunny, midday moment in Key West.

I biked back up through the Keys and visited Grossman Hammock State Park, in the Everglades, again. I arrived back at Barton Park, in Lake Worth, on March 11—camping once again at my secluded spot in the thick grove of palm trees, and gathering more coconuts to husk and eat.

There was a moment there that stands out. One night, well after dark, after I had set up camp in the grove, I was enjoying a solitude at the beach. The air was warm and the night was still, with a gentle surf. There was a full moon just beginning to rise over the ocean. The water sparkled from the full moon. It was a beautiful moment—and so peaceful.

The rest of the trip was just a lot of biking—up the east coast of Florida, through Georgia and South Carolina, into North Carolina— where I boxed up my bike and Bugger to send home and took a Greyhound Bus the rest of the way. I arrived back in *The Badger State* in late March—with an early April snowstorm welcoming me home to Wisconsin.

With the travel bug still biting, in the Fall I biked to Texas, Bugger and all, and wintered in Galveston—but that's a whole other adventure.

I'll close with a memory that has stayed with me through the years.

On Christmas Day, 1972, on my way to Florida—seven days into my solitary journey and a long way from home—I was pedaling along when a big black sedan passed me. The car slowed and the rear window rolled down and a little, dark-haired girl of about ten leaned out the window. With the prettiest bright eyes and the prettiest smile she called out to me, *"Merry Christmas!"*

That image has warmed my heart ever since. And now it can warm yours, too.

From our home to yours, blessings to each during this Christmas Season. And very best wishes for a Happy New Year. May 2019 bring peace and prosperity, health and happiness, to all.

Thought:
Thinking about doing something,
and actually doing it,
are two very different experiences.

Final thought:
"For God hath not given us
the spirit of fear;
but of power, and of love,
and of a sound mind."
2 Timothy 1:7 [KJV]

Afterword

Dear Friend,

Thank you for the welcome pleasure of your company during our adventure together in these pages. How was the journey?

I would love to hear from you. Allow me to invite your comments.

My email address is: vastark5@aol.com.

Thank you very kindly.

Sincerely,

Richard

San Francisco Book Review 2014—complete
(Prior to the addition of the ninth vignette, **A Florida Adventure**, in 2018)

Richard Stark's *WE ARE IN THIS TOGETHER: Reflections on the Dramas of Life* embodies a thoughtful, meditative work that captures the joy and sorrow felt throughout life. Stark's eight chapters break down into three reflective sections of family, patriotism, and self-reflection. The first section examines the loss of a parent, hope for a child, and the friends who become family over time. Stark's words prove tactful as well as enlightening. So many readers will relate to the loss of a friend or the precious time spent with a child.

In the next section, Stark studies nationalism and the impact of 9/11 on American daily life. Reading his account of that traumatic day, readers will find themselves thinking back to their own experiences. Everyone will remember the American flags that blanketed the United States. *"It is as though, with one accord, Americans everywhere are reaching for a security blanket—of red, white, and blue."*

Section three encompasses the personal journey each individual takes through life. The older one becomes, the faster time passes. In a blink of the eye, children return home fully-grown, dear friends pass away, and one cannot help but consider the path untaken. Stark's final chapter includes tips to help along his younger self, should a conversation have ever happened. His advice abounds with wisdom and understanding of a life fully lived. *"First, life is all about making choices. And we don't always choose wisely."* The younger readers will appreciate the guidance of Stark's words, and the older readers will find familiarity between his pages.

WE ARE IN THIS TOGETHER: Reflections on the Dramas of Life grasps the monumental aspects of life from specific moments to particular people. Earning four stars, it demonstrates a true appreciation for the path each individual must explore. The openness and empathy Stark's text exudes makes the work accessible to every reader and worth re-reading over the years to come.

Notes

Photographs were taken by the author.

The image of George Washington, and the photo of the Mount Vernon mansion, the home of our first president, were taken at the Mount Vernon National Historic Landmark, in Fairfax County, Virginia.

The cover photo, and the image of a seated James Madison holding a book with Dolly Madison standing behind him, and the photo of the Montpelier mansion, the home of the Madisons, were taken at the Montpelier National Historic Landmark, Orange County, Virginia. James Madison, our fourth president, drafted our United States Constitution.

The image of Thomas Jefferson, and the photo of the Jefferson Monticello home, were taken at the Monticello National Historic Landmark, Albemarle County, Virginia. Thomas Jefferson, author of the Declaration of Independence and founder of the University of Virginia, was our third president.

www.ingramcontent.com/pod-product-compliance
Lightning Source LLC
Chambersburg PA
CBHW061201070526
44579CB00009B/88